"An up-to-date account of how the response to the crisis is playing out and what this tells us about the changing nature of the UK state in a post-EU context."
Tony Heron, University of York

"I suspect we will be debating the impact of COVID-19 on the devolution settlement for years to come: Janice Morphet has provided an essential early survey of the issues."
Leighton Andrews, Cardiff Business School

T0335219

JANICE MORPHET

THE IMPACT OF COVID-19 ON DEVOLUTION

Recentralising the British State
Beyond Brexit?

BRISTOL
UNIVERSITY
PRESS

First published in Great Britain in 2021 by

Bristol University Press
University of Bristol
1-9 Old Park Hill
Bristol
BS2 8BB
UK
t: +44 (0)117 954 5940
e: bup-info@bristol.ac.uk

Details of international sales and distribution partners are available at
bristoluniversitypress.co.uk

British Library Cataloguing in Publication Data
A catalogue record for this book is available from the British Library

ISBN 978-1-5292-1620-2 paperback
ISBN 978-1-5292-1621-9 ePub
ISBN 978-1-5292-1622-6 ePdf

Cover design: Clifford Hayes
Front cover image: Scientist in coverall suit with a coronavirus
sample and British flag © prostooleh / Freepik
Bristol University Press uses environmentally responsible
print partners.
Printed and bound in Great Britain by CMP, Poole

Contents

Preface

Attempting to write a short book about COVID-19, Brexit and devolution when all are moving targets is a difficult proposition. The outcome from COVID-19 is as yet unknown, but what we see from the first moves to implement a mass vaccination programme replicates the centralised approaches used to manage the pandemic from its arrival in the UK in 2020, with a lack of transparency in how decisions are being made about who can be involved in making the jabs and how locations for vaccination have been selected. The weekly vaccination target numbers are given by the PM. But this time, the system has been operated, in plain sight, by the NHS not private contractors. The PM's popularity has increased through localism. Amidst this, the Trade Cooperation Agreement between the UK and the EU has been finalised and passed into law – except that it is hard to say that this is final – and there remain issues unresolved at the point of agreement, such as services, while other agreements will surely be changed as the experience of managing these agreed regimes become operational. What will the level playing field for regulation mean in practice? There may be political pressure for divergence but the business sector may lobby heavily to retain much of the pre-Brexit approach.

The opportunities for a post-Brexit evaluation of its effects on UK society may have to wait until we are in a post-COVID-19 world. This is when most people will start to experience the effects of the changes for travel and purchasing goods and services. There will also be a wider reckoning on the effects of the loss of the subsidiarity principle in GB – it still exists in Northern Ireland as part of the Protocol. The similarity of the two regimes on the island of Ireland and the differences between Northern Ireland and Scotland seem likely to exacerbate pressure for polls for reunification and independence, respectively. The economic benefits that Northern Ireland may gain from remaining within the EU will emphasise this widening difference.

The pandemic has also shown that the devolution settlement of the late 1990s failed to resolve the political and democratic leadership of England. Too often Westminster Ministers have talked about their UK policies when they have meant England. The COVID-19 pandemic has taught them and the media that the PM is first the leader of England before the leader of the UK. Yet in England, the centralised approach to managing the pandemic, that has left aside elected mayors and local authorities, has been significant. Coming after ten years of austerity policy, local government was not well-equipped to face the pandemic at the local level. However, as local leaders have seen the scale of COVID-19 funding passed to the private sector to undertake what has always been a local authority job, it has been sobering. Local government in England will emerge with more resolve for powers and independence than has been the case before. Perhaps the pandemic will only be tamed once the PM or his successor acknowledge the basic principles of managing public health crises – through the local level.

So, this book captures the debate at a particular point. After the pandemic, will democratic relationships resume their former patterns? This seems unlikely but there will be new matters in play – including a reform of Parliamentary boundaries, the strength of the changes in the newly won Conservative red wall constituencies, and public responses to Brexit in the airport queues. However, despite the changes brought by COVID-19 and as the country comes to terms with the effects of new post-Brexit processes, the underlying move to recentralise the state continues. This book is an opportunity to take stock of where we are and also, as in *Beyond Brexit* (Morphet 2017), to point out those policies and programmes that will continue to reinforce this objective.

As ever my thanks go to Emily Watt and all those at Bristol University Press that have helped to bring this book to life. The thoughts and views contained here are my own.

Janice Morphet

January 2021

List of Abbreviations

ADPH	Association of Directors of Public Health
BIC	British-Irish Council
CEC	Commission of the European Communities
COBRA	Cabinet Office Briefing Rooms
CoR	Committee of the Regions
CRG	COVID Recovery Group
DBEIS	Department for Business, Energy & Industrial Strategy
DExEU	Department for Exiting the European Union
DfID	Department for International Development
DHSC	Department of Health and Social Care
DUP	Democratic Unionist Party
EC	European Commission
ECJ	European Court of Justice
EU	European Union
FCDO	Foreign, Commonwealth & Development Office
FEA	Functional Economic Area
FM	First Minister
FUA	Functional Urban Area
GATT	General Agreement on Tariffs and Trades
GDP	Gross Domestic Product
GFA	Good Friday Agreement
GLA	Greater London Authority
GP	General Practitioner
HMG	Her Majesty's Government
ICU	Intensive Care Unit
IfG	Institute for Government
IPS	Infection Prevention Society
JBS	Joint Biosecurity Centre
JMC	Joint Ministerial Council
JR	Judicial Review
LEP	Local Enterprise Partnership

LGA	Local Government Association
LOCB	Local Outbreak Control Boards
LRF	Local Resilience Forum
MCA	Mayoral Combined Authority
MHCLG	Ministry of Housing, Communities & Local Government
MLG	Multi-Level Governance
NAO	National Audit Office
OBR	Office for Budget Responsibility
OECD	Organisation for Economic Cooperation and Development
OEP	Office of Environmental Protection
PHE	Public Health England
PHW	Public Health Wales
PM	Prime Minister
PPE	personal protective equipment
RDA	Regional Development Agency
RSA	Royal Society for the Arts, Manufactures and Commerce
SAGE	Scientific Advisory Group for Emergencies
SCG	Strategic Coordination Group
SME	Small and Medium Enterprise
TfEU	Treaty for the European Union
TTT	test, track and trace
WHO	World Health Organization
WTO	World Trade Organization

ONE

Devolution in the UK: The Twin Challenges of Brexit and COVID-19

Introduction

The onset of COVID-19 has highlighted not only the Government's ill-preparedness for the pandemic across the UK but also how much of the Whitehall machine is only responsible for England. Since 1999, there has been very little acknowledgement of the devolved national administrations in Scotland, Wales and Northern Ireland within the UK Government and Whitehall (Cheung et al 2019). There have been few constitutional or machinery of government changes that have reflected the increasing depth of devolution in practice (Leyland 2011; McEwen et al 2020). There are few formal mechanisms for coordination and liaison with the UK Government through more regular contact between the governments of the three devolved nations (Clifford and Morphet 2015). This is in part because there is no separation for Government Ministers between their UK and English responsibilities. The slippage in their language often elides and confuses their responsibilities for England with those of the UK (Cushion et al 2020).

The COVID-19 pandemic in the UK has changed this. It is now transparent that the Prime Minister (PM), Boris Johnson, is PM of England and the powers devolved across health, the economy, culture and local government are different in each of the four nations. The PM has demonstrated the lack of understanding of these differences through his actions and attitudes towards the First Ministers (FMs) of the nations with devolved administrations, who have taken a much more proactive and cautious approach to managing the pandemic than has been the case for England. However, the PM has subsequently copied their initiatives – including for school closures, examination results, wearing of face coverings and lockdowns. Douglas Ross MP, the leader of the Scottish Conservative Party, that is separate from the party in the rest of the UK, said on BBC Radio 4's Today programme (2 November 2020) said that he wanted to see both governments working together to support Scotland through the pandemic – recognising the reality of the structure of the UK state.

At the same time in England, there have been similar tensions and confrontations between the PM and directly elected Labour Mayors in Liverpool, Manchester and London (Denham 2020a). In October 2020, these confrontations were concerned with the declaration of tiered lockdowns enforced by the Government, supported by imposed 'deals' rather than the application of common criteria across the country. In London, after being requested by the Government to significantly reduce the operation of Transport for London (TfL), the Mayor of London, Sadiq Khan has been accused of profligacy and the Government has threatened to remove the Mayor's powers over TfL as a consequence of his alleged 'mismanagement' of the budget during the pandemic (Pickard 2020). The PM has also been moving to reorganise English local government into larger units and, simultaneously, to fundamentally change the legal basis of one of their main functions, that of planning (MHCLG 2020). This is at the same time as managing the implementation of Brexit. This appears to be taking on a much bigger policy load than the Government can manage. Yet, looking back to when the UK joined the EU in 1972, exactly the same policy pattern was the case, with reform of the planning system in 1968–70 and of local government in 1972 (Morphet 2013).

While there has been a practical disregard for the devolved nations in the management of the pandemic, the PM has also been handling the negotiations with the UK's exit from the

EU. In this there has been an approach to creating a single market within the UK which has not only been marked by the PM's intentions to break international law (Payne et al 2020) in relation to the Northern Ireland Protocol (2019), a treaty agreed between the UK and EU as part of Brexit, but has also included what has been described as a 'power grab' (Torrance 2020) to return devolved powers to the central state in London. However, what has been less noticed is that this recentralisation was not a new move but one which had been gathering pace since 2016 (Wincott 2018). First evidenced in the Wales Bill 2015 (Sandford and Gormley Heaton 2020), the May Government removed some of the devolved powers through the European Union Withdrawal Act 2018 and launched the Dunlop Review of the UK Government Union capability to consider the increasing role of Whitehall in the devolved nations (May 2019; HMG 2019a). This position was reinforced in the Queen's speech published by the PM after the 2019 general election (HMG 2019b) and has been exacerbated by the growing opinion poll results in favour of independence in Scotland during the pandemic (Gilbert and Clark 2020). At the same time, less on the radar, the Treasury has been undertaking more financial undermining of the devolved powers through the use of deals made directly with the local authorities in Scotland, Wales and Northern Ireland whereby preselected projects from London are exchanged for direct funding (Jones et al 2017). In local government in England, these 'deals' have centralised funding and project selection through the diversion of funding from local authorities into Local Enterprise Partnerships (LEPs) (Pike et al 2013). In the Spending Review 2020 (Sunak 2020) it was announced that the allocation of these 'levelling up' projects would be made in Whitehall for the whole of the UK, and that approval for each project would be made by the Member of Parliament (MP). This has been described as a further indication of the PM's use of 'pork barrel' or clientalist politics to channel funds to Conservative voting or marginal seats, as in the Towns Fund (Syal 2020d).

This book examines the intertwined relationships between the PM's management of the COVID-19 pandemic, Brexit and the policy objectives to recentralise the UK state by removing powers from devolved administrations and reforming English local government into larger units. In this, the PM is using both episodes to reclaim the union (Kenny and Sheldon 2020). After Brexit, there is no legal basis on which to protect the devolved institutional future of the UK nations and English local government beyond the period of the current Parliament. Devolution has not been enshrined in the British constitution or in a reformed House of Lords. Devolved powers have been resting on the principle of subsidiarity in EU treaties which were removed on 1 January 2021, and on the UK leaving the EU this legal protection for UK devolution is also removed (Morphet 2017). The timing of events has been significant (Goetz and Mayer-Sahling 2009) as COVID-19 has strengthened practical devolution at the time when it is most in danger of being undermined and reduced through Brexit. The book discusses these issues by considering the handling of the COVID-19 pandemic at three governance scales – state, national and local – and will discuss the longer-term implications of this temporal collision of issues for the UK state.

While the pressure to recentralise the UK has been apparent since 2015, the momentum has increased with the opportunities provided by the statecraft associated with Brexit. At the same time, the pandemic has allowed the role and differentiation of the devolved nations to emerge more clearly. While Mount (2020a) states that reducing the influence of devolution has been a long-held ambition of the Conservative Party, on 16 November 2020 the PM told a group of MPs for the North of England that devolution in Scotland had been 'disastrous' and the worst mistake made by the Blair government (Brooks et al 2020). Since the General Election in 2019, the Government has been more presidential in style, focusing on the PM rather than being led by the Cabinet (Mount 2020b), further centralising power.

Why does the Government want to recentralise power?

In examining the reasons why the PM and Whitehall have adopted strategies to recentralise the UK state and to reduce the powers available to the devolved nations as a result of Brexit, Dahlström et al (2011) suggest that this is part of a common process in western democratic governments. They argue that these governments were in support of 'letting go' of power – through devolution and liberalisation of public services – only to find that this brought challenges in the management of the state. As a consequence, Dahlström et al (2011) argue that western governments shifted their approach to 'holding on' to power and then have acted to 'restore the centre'. How have each of these three stages of recentralisation operated within the UK?

I: Letting go

Dahlström et al (2011) argue that devolution, decentralisation, and liberalisation in the public sector were regarded as a 'good thing' (2011: 4). Decentralisation and liberalisation have been a more persistent narrative in the post-1945 British state (Smith 1985) than in other countries that have devolved more responsibilities, such as France, Spain and Denmark (Page 1991). In part, these 'letting go' narratives – 'steering' and not 'rowing' (Osborne and Gaebler 1993) – were a mechanism to provide policy cover for the implementation of the liberalisation of the public sector through the GATT agreements in 1980, 1988 and 1994 (Morphet 2021a). Here, the public sector role in service delivery was reclassified as 'enabling', allowing wider public service reforms to be associated with these outsourcing agreements through statecraft. Letting go through decentralisation can also be seen as a means of supporting cultural and spatial differentiation within the state (Camões 2020). Further, the work of Krugman (1991), taken forward by the OECD and the EU, suggests that aligning the boundaries of Functional

Economic Areas (FEAs) with strong governance results in a positive increase in national GDP and as a mode to be pursued (Ahrend et al 2014; Charbit 2020).

'Letting go' is not a passive role for the state but a rules-based approach, using common standards which could release more focus on policy at the centre. However, there are political and financial costs of decentralisation (Camões 2020), as demonstrated in the effects of outsourcing in the UK, that have created a leadership deficit (Morphet 2021a). Whitehall considered that outsourcing was a mechanism for establishing more control through the use of contractors (Theakston, 2016; Rhodes 2018) but soon realised that these institutional reforms made it more difficult to implement long-term change if delivery was set within contractual arrangements. Accountability was also more difficult to locate. Decentralisation may have benefits but it also reached a point where it created costs (Camões 2020).

The introduction of devolution in the UK in 1999 was the second means of 'letting go'. It provided a mechanism for the devolved administrations to determine the delivery of EU legislation and projects but not to shape them through direct negotiation. However, while the UK Government has used the language of devolution to contain the overriding narrative of increased sub-state power for the UK nations, it has implemented decentralisation. There are similarities and differences in these terms, and while decentralisation has frequently been used to describe institutional reforms in France (Thoenig 2005; Cole 2006), it has not been used in the UK. Decentralisation is an organising principle that is applied to the level within the state where issues are managed and resolved (Pollitt et al 2016). However, as the history of local government within the UK demonstrates, decentralisation is not accompanied by devolution of power to determine how these decisions are taken – it is an administrative rather than a government tool (MacKinnon 2015; Lowndes and Gardner 2016). In the absence of a written constitution, the pattern of decentralised administration in England is haphazard, reflecting prevailing considerations for operational convenience within Whitehall at the time of legislative drafting (Chandler 2013). Hence, some institutional procedures are local within a strongly defined national framework, such as the registration of births, deaths and marriages, while decisions on planning applications are considered locally within a national legal framework, with a national disputes procedure that can be overridden by government ministers.

Devolution has provided a legal and democratic framework for the application of subsidiarity within which decisions are made at what is considered to be the appropriate scale of government (Bannink and Ossewaarde 2012), although this has challenges (Smoke 2015). The power to determine raising and allocating resources is a principal component of devolution and separates it from decentralisation (Heald and MacLeod 2002; Greer 2005). The pressures and application of devolutionary practices in Scotland, Wales and Northern Ireland have not been enshrined in the UK constitution, leaving an uneasy relationship between their administrations and the UK central state (McEwen et al 2020). The implementation of devolution in this sense has proved to be particularly difficult within the UK, which has no written constitution (Trench 2007; McHarg and Mitchell 2017). The application of the process of the legislative consent motions through the Sewel Convention 'applies when the UK Parliament legislates on a matter which is devolved to the Scottish Parliament. It holds that this will happen only if the Scottish Parliament has given its consent' (Bowers 2005: 1) and has been extended to the other devolved administrations but is not enforceable in law (Anthony 2018).

The lack of clarity over the difference between English and UK powers has caused ambivalence for UK politicians on the scope of their reach and for civil servants' operational practices. This can be illustrated by the role of Government ministers who serve both the UK and England. Although academics and commentators have suggested projecting bounded definitions of devolution onto the UK constitution, it has remained untouched in its core structure (Brazier 2001; Oliver 2003; Mitchell 2004; Hazell 2005; Cabinet Office 2012). This is also in stark comparison with other EU member states where sub-state democratic structures are included within constitutions (Hooghe et al 2001; Morphet 2013). While the UK has been a member of the EU, the treaties have provided an overarching framework and supra-legal role in relation to domestic legislation in those policy areas that have been pooled by the UK within the EU, for example, transport, energy, environment and rural affairs. The operation of the EU's core principles of subsidiarity, fairness and equality between places, known as 'cohesion', have been set out in its successive treaties and supported by cumulative legislation. To be compliant with these agreements, the UK has introduced devolutionary practices without formally acknowledging or accepting them as changes to the UK constitution (McHarg 2018). This hybrid fluidity reflects the UK's uneasy relationship with the shared competences it has had within its membership of the EU (Morphet 2017).

The absence of the UK's core adoption of these EU principles has been submerged (Leyland 2011). This can be illustrated by the failure of the UK to engage fully in the British-Irish Council (BIC) that was established with the intention of regularly bringing together the leaders of each part of the UK (Lynch and Hopkins 2001; Coakley 2014; Trench 2015). There has also been a failure to consistently include the political leaders for Scotland, Wales and Northern Ireland in UK central Government decision making in an open way, with the views of the devolved nations continuing to be represented in London by Whitehall Departments and centrally appointed Secretaries of State for their territories. The mechanism of the Joint Ministerial Council (JMC) has not been used consistently (McEwen et al 2020). Opportunities to change the nature of this democratic representation through reform of the House of Lords have been evaded (Norton 2017). The term for the governments in Scotland, Wales and Northern Ireland that is used in Whitehall of devolved administrations, reflects a similar basis as local authorities, as legal but not constitutional entities.

II: Holding on

In response to finding that 'letting go' had unanticipated challenges, Dahlström et al (2011) suggest that the next approach adopted for institutional design in government was 'holding on'. This maintained the power at the centre of the state while giving the outward impression that the state was letting go. The increased use of agencification and public private partnerships (PPPs) were mechanisms for holding on to power that were also able to be used for political ends (Morphet 2021a). However, this too has been problematic. Agencies may be too unwieldy to respond to central government sponsors or political signals (Egeberg and Trondal 2009). Moynihan (2006) also argues that these ideas are transferred between the civil services of different nations without considering whether there is a good fit to their methods of government. Experience in the UK has shown that agencies can be liberalised and then taken back inside Whitehall, such as border control and the probation service (Morphet 2021a).

While most of the application of decentralisation practices in the UK has been in Scotland, Wales and Northern Ireland, less consideration has been given to the application of the principles of fairness, subsidiarity and territorial cohesion within England. There have been some calls for an English Parliament but these have not attracted a movement to support its creation (Hazell 2006; Russell and Sheldon 2018). In Scotland and Wales, local government reorganisation in the 1990s was used as a prelude to changing decision-making procedures that subsequently supported devolution practices. The position in England outside London was very different. Here local government reorganisation 1990–97 was used to reinforce centralised decision making through the creation of quasi-democratic institutional structures across England – including Government Offices, Regional Assemblies and Regional Development Agencies (RDAs) (Pemberton and Morphet 2014). The scale of these English reforms enabled the UK to argue that, at least in the short term, decision making on EU programmes and domestic expenditure was being devolved to regional level.

However, from 1992 onwards each passage of institutional reform in English governance, including the abolition of these newly-formed regional institutions, by both Labour and Coalition Governments, was made to retain central control. Within the devolved administrations and English local government, through the extension of subsidiarity principles in the Lisbon Treaty 2009, the UK Government was required to devolve its powers and funding to the lowest appropriate level of decision making (Pazos-Vidal 2019). However, this was not an approach that was welcome in Whitehall. When it became clear that the EC would be pressurising the UK Government to allocate central funding and decision-making powers on EU programmes to local democratic bodies, as the terms of the territorial cohesion principles require (Barca 2009), the Government established new forms of institutionalised 'holding on' at the local level in England.

The LEPs were established from 2010 onwards with no legislative underpinning (Sandford 2013). While the format of the establishment of the LEPs used the language of bottom-up self-determination of the LEP areas, they have never been democratically accountable (Willett 2016; Blunkett et al 2016) and defined as a continuation of RDAs (Marlow 2019). The Government channelled both the EU cohesion programmes and its own form of centralised localism in project and programme delivery through them, although a Government commitment to decentralised democratic decision making was made through the establishment of Mayoral Combined Authorities (MCAs) (Osborne 2014) and the use of 'deals'. Centrally determined programmes were passed through a wide-mesh sieve of local agreement.

The Government stated that this funding was to be spent on locally determined projects, but LEPs and 'deals' had no legal basis and no accountability to local democratically elected local authorities, as a Government review demonstrated (Ney 2018). This has moved the relationship between central and local government in England to a transactional basis. Longstanding local authority revenue support grants were tapered out by 2020 and replaced by a 'deal' culture. These growth, devolution, city and town deals appear as contractual forms between the Government and local authorities – individually or in groups, vertically or horizontally. The Government sets the terms for the 'deal' offers and local authorities are then required to bid for them within controlled priorities (O'Brien and Pike 2015). In practice, these are centrally-driven programmes and there are no local powers of choice (Sandford 2017) acting as top-down control within 'the shadow of hierarchy' (Héritier and Lehmkuhl 2008; Reichborn-Kjennerud and Vabo 2017). This deal culture has become the normal central/local working relationship. Local authorities have had to engage as their funding has been cut through austerity (Lowndes and Gardner 2016; NAO 2019). It has also meant that local authorities have been seeking new ways of achieving financial independence outside this reliance on deals set within central Government priorities (Morphet and Clifford 2020).

While this 'deal' culture has been examined and shown not to have reinforced devolutionary practices within England (Ayres et al 2018), its relationship to strategies that are designed to evade the application of subsidiarity have not been made. Rather, they have been aligned to the prevailing political ideology of governments, without considering the extent to which they present a continuing narrative of the retention of central power, meeting Kingdon's (2013) agenda-setting principles test. The UK central Government, through the role of the Cabinet Office, has a longstanding track record of using its advanced knowledge of EU policy and legislative programmes to manage the domestic agenda in anticipation of these changes (Wilke and Wallace 1990), through a process of longtail statecraft. Even where there is an acknowledgement that there has been a requirement to address subsidiarity, those appointed to advise on reform have acknowledged them but felt powerless to act (Grant 1993). While deals are a means of controlling local expenditure, there have been suggestions that it has made local government 'blame takers' for this austerity. Local authority leaders have consistently suggested that the importance of the deals lay not in their current initial content but in their potential to evolve in the future (Ayres et al 2018: 860). However, deals have made local authorities more dependent on the central state.

III: Restoring the centre

The last move in recentralisation is to 'restore the centre', where there is an increase in strategic capacity to 'restore the primacy of politics' (Dahlström et al 2011: 16) in decision making and policy presentation. In the UK, there appears to be a view growing at the centre of Government that devolution has gone 'too far' (Solar and Smith 2020; Brookes et al 2020) and there is a need to return to a unified state (May 2019; HMG 2019a). Devolution does not sit easily with a 'first past the post' electoral system as the UK remains one of the most centralised states (OECD 2020a). Now the UK has left the EU, there are no constraints on the Government's legal programme within the constitution and the sovereignty of Parliament. Other centralising activities in the UK have included the expansion of the PM's office when led by Dominic Cummings (Blunkett and Flinders 2020), who also proposed the reform of the civil service (Maddox 2020). This perception of a need for more centralised control has also been found in Germany, where more power has been created by building up central departments (Fleischer 2011).

In the UK, after using a range of methods (Harris and Rutter 2015) including the Prime Minister's Strategy and Delivery Units, and the increasing role of the Cabinet Office (Seldon and Meakin 2016), Prime Minister May started to address recentralisation through the establishment of the Dunlop Review (HMG 2019a). The Queen's Speech (2019) repeated the policy of reinforcing Whitehall's role in the Union. The UK Government's response to Brexit has also included a range of legal initiatives that will serve to reduce the process of devolution and remake the constitution 'under our noses' (Wincott 2018; Baldini et al 2018; Sykes 2018).

This recentralisation is occurring despite the populist orthodoxy of Brexit being a 'bottom-up' movement (Richards and Smith 2017; Richards et al 2019). The Government's approach accords with the loose devolution settlement that has prevailed in the UK since its inception. Sandford and Gormley-Heenan (2020) argue that no other course of action could be anticipated within these arrangements to ensure a smooth Brexit transition. The UK Government has argued devolved powers should be held centrally for a period. In the European Union (Withdrawal) Act 2018, the devolved powers for environment, transport, agriculture and energy were recentralised (McEwen and Redmond 2019; Keating 2019). Initially it was proposed that this would have no time limit, although a review mechanism of three years was inserted, without any commitment to its implementation. The Withdrawal Agreement Act 2019 also included proposals for a significant extension of the role of Henry Vlll powers that would allow governments to pass legislation without reference to Parliament, increasing the power of the executive and minimising the opportunity for any amendment. The Government has also failed to use the legislative consent motion process. Although a convention, rather than a legal requirement, the FMs of Scotland and Wales wrote to the Prime Minister on 22 October 2019 to request that the Withdrawal Agreement Bill be subject to this process, but were ignored.

The absence of engagement with the devolved administrations in Scotland and Wales since the 2016 Brexit referendum has been a source of frustration to their governments (McEwen et al 2020). In Northern Ireland, the confidence and supply relationship between the Government and the DUP did not survive. The Withdrawal Agreement, including the Northern Ireland Protocol, arguably means that a temporary back-stop arrangement for customs on the island of Ireland has become permanent and is now located in the Irish Sea. This is unacceptable to the DUP, completing the alienation of all three devolved administrations, even before the PM's 'devolution has been a disaster' remarks (Brooks et al 2020). As Wincott et al (2017) identified, there would be consequences for the practices and processes of devolution within the UK as a result of Brexit, and here it is argued that centralisation is a strategic objective being pursued by the UK state, and is facilitated further by it.

While these institutional changes have emerged in the preparations for Brexit since 2016, the role of the EU in creating the conditions for devolution in the UK has been pivotal. Brexit provides an opportunity to unwind devolution which was already coming under pressure. It introduces a further dilemma about the future of the UK state following Brexit (Wincott 2017). The role of the devolved administrations after Brexit has not been discussed. They have been promised more powers (Honeycombe-Foster 2020; Torrance 2020) but the details are not explicit and, following this Government statement, the UK Internal Market Bill included provisions to remove further powers. This has been described as a 'power grab' (Dougan et al 2020). The processes of devolution in the UK have rested on EU treaties. If the UK is no longer party to these, then the Scottish and Welsh Parliaments and Northern Ireland Assemblies will require a new legislative mandate. Furthermore, without any constitutional reform, the Parliament and Assemblies have only the guarantee for their life of the term of that Parliament, as no Parliament can fetter any future Parliament's decisions (Trench 1993). This matter has not been recognised nor discussed as part of the public Brexit debate.

In England, 'restoring the centre' through LEPs has been reinforced as they have become non-departmental public bodies and direct successors of RDAs (MHCLG 2017). Further, some of the expenditure powers devolved to the Mayor of London for housing have now been recentralised and are subject to the Secretary of State's control for the first time in 20 years. The Government has not made any specific proposals for further recentralising the state in England, although four new regional twitter accounts for HMG have been established. These regions have not been defined in any formal way but have emerged in the Kerslake (2020) UK2070 Commission where four regions have been proposed in England, giving the UK seven regions in all. The Royal Society of Arts's One Powerhouse project (RSA 2019) has also provided regional plans for each of these four regions that were launched on the same day as the first stage of the Kerslake Review (RSA 2021). Finally, in England the move to a more centralised regional decision making has been made in a Labour Party policy discussion paper and builds on this approach. While no formal statements have been made by the Government, there have been indications by civil servants about taking a more central and leading role in policy and re-establishing regional offices and links (Gallagher 2019).

This approach to four regions in England differs from the traditional approaches adopted in the 1930s, based on nine regions (Glasson and Marshall 2007). In these, the scale and dominance of the South-East region's population size and economy have always been considered an issue that leads to an unbalanced outcome for all English regions. In One Powerhouse (RSA 2021), the sizes of the territories in the four regions are similar, while their economic and demographic profiles vary. A UK shift to four regions in England supports a stronger central state. With larger, more strategic regions, central government can argue that the relationships with them are at a more appropriate scale and it can then distance its relationship with local government. This gives space for both meeting EU subsidiarity commitments, should they continue to be required in any post-Brexit agreement, and the OECD (2020a) economic policy recommendations. Indeed, the OECD arguments about the relationship between governance and economic performance in FEAs is given as an argument for the Government's proposed policy for devolution (HMG 2019a). At the same time, it allows much greater movement between Whitehall officials and these four large, strategic regional bodies to support influence and decision making. This will be particularly the case if these regions have no democratic bodies to which they are accountable.

In the establishment of new regional bodies, the directly-elected mayors of the recently formed combined authorities may be opposed to their new powers being taken upwards to another governance scale. This tension could allow a non-democratic structure to remain in place for some time. An alternative approach, through the establishment of an English Parliament, is also problematic, as is the reform of the House of Lords to comprise sub-state representatives, which would be opposed by the House of Commons. There is little support for any of these rescaling initiatives but the size of the PM's majority in Parliament after the 2019 General Election will mean that any Government preferred proposals will be implemented. Further, as the Scottish and Welsh Parliaments have already found, their lack of a constitutional anchor provides them with no protection or security against five-year Parliamentary decision making in the UK's episodic system.

The opportunity of COVID-19: the battle between centralisation and devolution

The actions being taken to recentralise decision making in the UK state appear to be more intentional than randomly taken. As discussed in other chapters, the PM's management of COVID-19 has deployed a number of tools of bringing power to the centre, through the use of privatised providers rather than local authorities, cronyism for appointments and the politicisation of local lockdowns. However, the PM has not been able to control the devolved administrations and this has demonstrated a weakness in his centralisation strategy, which he has attempted to remedy through Brexit.

TWO

Central Government, Brexit and COVID-19: Centralisation Through Privatisation?

What is the role of the government in national crises?

The roles and responsibilities of state governments are to anticipate crises and then to provide safe and secure ways through the episode to restore normality. There are also increasing public and business expectations that governments should be able to prevent these crises or ameliorate them as quickly as possible by mobilising resources or reorganising its own actions and priorities, as in the 2008 international financial crisis. There is also a growing understanding, after 40 years of globalisation, that the episodes that occur in one part of the world will have effects elsewhere (OECD 2017). This has been the case of COVID-19 where governments have had to intervene to manage the effects of the pandemic and attempt to reduce its spread (NAO 2020a).

In considering the roles of government, in anticipating and responding to major crises that affect the state, the primary requirement is that of leadership, the deployment of assets and management of the transition to a more acceptable way of life, even if this is not the same as that before the emergency occurred. In considering the management of health risks, public health strategies have consistently required people to change their habits and behaviours, with investment in public infrastructure such as clean water and through a regulatory environment that has reinforced these standards. However, despite these, there can be disasters which are regarded as having a major political dimension such as the Grenfell Tower fire (Macleod 2018) and corporate failure in rail accidents (Machin and Mayr 2013). Increasing regulatory standards are a consistent government response to disasters, taking the lessons learned and applying them. At the same time, the business environment is constantly attempting to reduce regulatory standards, through lobbying government (Davidson 2017) and regarding them as costs (McGregor-Lowndes and Ryan 2009).

The public sector at all scales of government are responders of last resort when crises occur within their spheres of responsibility. In the UK, the pressures on all public sector budgets in the period of austerity since 2010 (Gamble 2015; Morphet and Clifford 2020) have inevitably led to service reductions and, in some cases, complete cuts (NAO 2018). By using processes such as 'value engineering' and 'lean' methods (Radnor and Walley 2008), projects and services are reviewed with the intention of cutting costs and, at times, this can be without paying sufficient attention to the spirit and letter of the regulatory environment which supports public safety.

How has the UK central Government managed crises before COVID-19?

Since the 1990s, most of the attention on managing UK crises has been focused on defence and security, particularly in relation to home-grown terror incidents. Other major crises have been the effects of foot and mouth disease (Gregory 2005), the oil tanker drivers' strike in 1999 (Doherty et al 2003), and flooding (Hendry et al 2019). These emergencies have had significant effects on large parts of the country and highlighted the weakness of systems dependent on 'just in time' delivery methods. Other crises have been equally important in terms of their effects but have not had the same level of visibility in the public domain, including the number of influenza deaths each year, the rising concerns about social care, and food poverty among those with low incomes.

In order to prepare for crises, the Government undertakes regular reviews, provides a rating for each risk identified, and produces a national risk assessment (Cabinet Office 2017). Over time, some new risks have emerged for the securitisation of energy supply (Judge and Maltby 2017), cyberattacks (Stoddart 2016) and biosecurity (McLeish and Nightingale 2007; Home Office 2018). There are also lessons learned from past events, including political management and communication (McConnell 2003; Gregory 2005; NAO 2019), as well as mobilising resources (NAO 2013). For each risk, the Government undertakes planning, including gaming the effects of specific types of incidents. The response to the terror attack in London on 7/7 2005 was based on this kind of preparation, although this does not appear to have been in place at the time of the Manchester Arena bombing in 2019 (Craigie et al 2020). In the UK, there was a three-day risk assessment trial for a biosecurity pandemic, Operation Cygnus, as part of this process in 2016. The conclusions were not made public until October 2020 after public pressure (Pegg 2020). Operation Cygnus should have provided the Government with an opportunity to prepare procedures, stocks of medicines and equipment, and public communications strategies to respond if such an event took place, but they were wound down (NAO 2020e). Local authorities also have emergency plans and training to support their responses to the most likely risks that they face including flooding, transport accidents or incidents, or fire damage to critical infrastructure.

For health emergencies the Government has established the Scientific Advisory Group for Emergencies (SAGE), which is a standing group of those in medicine and other fields such as science, anthropology and psychology who provide advice to the Government. This includes what might happen in a pandemic, how it might be managed and how the public's responses and behaviours can be influenced to reduce the effects on society. SAGE also advises on changes in behaviour such as panic buying of food (Manderson and Levine 2020) and the acceptability of wearing face coverings (Greenhalgh 2020). When a major civil incident occurs at national level, the PM calls a meeting of COBRA, an acronym of the Cabinet Office Briefing Rooms that has been used as a term for crisis meetings in a national emergency (Freedman 2020). COBRA brings together those managing the crisis including Ministers, the police, and other emergency services. Since devolution in 1999, they will also generally include the FMs of the devolved nations and the Mayor of London. These COBRA meetings may be on a daily basis while the crisis is growing and at its peak. The PM may not attend all meetings and may delegate responsibility to senior Ministers.

Other approaches for longer-lasting issues that have a signifi-cant effect on managing change or threats to the country can be through the use of the machinery of government, that is to restructure Whitehall to manage the changes in the longer term (McConnell 2003; Page 2010). However, this has not been used in any consistent way. At the time of devolution, in 1999, the Government maintained the same structures and relied upon much of the machinery of government established through the Good Friday Agreement (GFA) for liaison and working across the four nations in the BIC and within the UK, through the JMC (Lynch and Hopkins 2001; McEwen et al 2020). However, there was never any attempt to change the way in which the state is structured, for example by including the three nations into the constitution. The role of the three gov-ernment offices for the nations was reduced but not removed, leaving a lingering central thread of a relationship between the UK Government and the FMs.

In contrast to this, the machinery of government has been used to respond to other major changes, including Brexit and international aid commitments, when the Department for International Development (DfID) was established in 1997. This marked a change in government policy backed by an ongoing commitment to aid from the UK that was fixed at 0.7% of GDP. This was seen as a positive move and represented the position of the UK internationally, and was in place between 1997 and 2020. The second major creation of a new Department was that for Exiting the EU (DExEU) which was in place from July 2016, immediately after the Brexit referendum. DExEU's role was to coordinate negotiations with the EU on the final Brexit trade deal and also to prepare for the effects on the UK of a range of political outcomes including 'no deal'. What is interesting about these new Departments, established to manage the UK's changing position in the world, is that they were both short-lived and eventually fell prey to the interests of more longstanding departments. The FCDO was the main beneficiary after languishing in a backwater since the Brexit referendum. The Brexiteers considered the FCDO to be in the remain camp. The appointment of Boris Johnson as Foreign Secretary in the May Government (2016–18) was a nod to these concerns. By having a 'Vote Leave' Secretary of State, it was considered as a means to keep the FCDO under control, and through the appointment of Johnson, simultaneously to demonstrate that it was not regarded as a central and serious department.

UK approaches to a pandemic within a global context

The UK recognises the international role and lead of the WHO to support states in dealing with pandemics. The OECD also shares information and best practice to support its members. While 2020 was a year when the UK was in transitional arrangements to leave the EU on 31 December, it also remained a member. The UK decided to withdraw from EU decision-making processes and meetings but still operated within its legal framework. The EU acted in response to the effects of the pandemic on the economies of member states, agreeing a series of soft measures on the management of state aid so that business could be provided with support packages. At the same time, the European Commission (EC) put together a consortium to procure personal protective equipment (PPE) and vaccines. There were continuing concerns about the UK's lack of adequate PPE, and its failure to respond to opportunities to be part of the EU's procurement framework was regarded as motivated by politics rather than public safety. There were a variety of reasons for this advanced in the media, including that the email inviting the UK to participate had been lost or was languishing on a junior official's computer. Eventually, there was an acknowledgement that this failure to respond in time to join the EU consortium opportunities had been a political act (BBC 2020b).

The Prime Minister's response to COVID-19

From the outset, the PM took an approach to managing the emerging pandemic in ways that were different from those used before. The PM delayed taking any action, centralised the response, privatised solutions and politicised the management of the crisis, using different approaches according to the party political affiliations of directly-elected mayors and council leaders (Stafford 2020). These approaches are discussed in more detail below.

I: Personalisation

The PM adopted a personalised approach to managing the pandemic from the outset. It was part of a more presidential style of government that Dahlström et al (2011) identified as being the last stage of 'restoring the centre'. Earlier, to reinforce this personalisation in his style of leadership, the PM required all Conservative Parliamentary candidates to sign an agreement to support Brexit before being adopted in the 2019 General Election. Recentralisation was accelerated by the adoption of emergency powers in the Coronavirus Act 2020 that enabled the PM to act without any other Parliamentary approval or pre-decision scrutiny. These emergency powers were taken after a delay in the PM's recognition of the scale and potential seriousness of the COVID-19 pandemic and its likely effects on the UK. In delaying the introduction of the first period of lockdown in England, the PM reacted later than actions taken in Scotland and Wales. In part this delay was on the basis of advice offered by the PM's then political adviser, Dominic Cummings, who was said to have argued for a strategy of herd immunity – that is where high numbers of people are infected, so that this provides some cover for the spread across the population as a whole (Scambler 2020). The PM's delay was also in part due to a misdiagnosis of the type of virus that was the basis of COVID-19. In the UK it was described as being like influenzas with similar symptoms and as a virus that would not affect most people. If advice had been sought from the WHO and those countries in South-East Asia that had COVID-19 first, then the diagnosis of a virus closer to SARS and its attendant consequences would have been established.

The PM also implemented delays in order to assess the political response to proposed actions throughout his management of the COVID-19 pandemic, using this as an operational strategy (Wardman 2020). These delays were part of the centralisation strategy which prioritised the NHS over care homes (Daly 2020). The delays in the requirement to wear a face covering in public places, public transport and secondary schools were later than those in Scotland in each case. The decision to hold a second lockdown in England in November 2020 came after the PM's advisers had requested this in September and after Wales, Scotland and Northern Ireland had implemented their own lockdowns which, in the case of Wales and Scotland, prohibited cross-border movements to and from England at different times.

In each case, the delays in the PM's actions appear to be taken as his decision rather than after Cabinet discussion and in response to party political objections. Within the Conservative Party, growing antagonism to the PM's approach on each of the issues that he has delayed has continued to reduce his Parliamentary majority, although opinion polls have demonstrated public support for lockdown (Ipsos MORI 2020). The PM faced major opposition from his own back-bench MPs, including from the chair of the 1922 Committee, Sir Graham Brady, to an extension of the emergency powers (White 2020). Sir Graham's campaign was headed off by assurances given by the PM that he would bring back further such decisions to Parliament where they affected the whole country, but the PM did not apply this commitment when he immediately announced a wide range of local lockdowns and then a second period of English lockdown four weeks later.

The PM also contracted COVID-19 and spent time in St Thomas' Hospital and later, in November 2020 had to isolate after failing to observe social distancing in a meeting with Northern MPs, after one tested positive for the disease. While the PM has exhorted others to act in a responsible way, his own actions together with those of his adviser Dominic Cummings, who travelled to Durham and then Barnard Castle during the first English lockdown, have reduced the level of public confidence in his leadership (Cuthbertson 2020).

II: Centralisation

One of the overriding features of the way in which the PM has approached the management of the pandemic that was different from any that had gone before, was the centralisation of the response (Mount 2020b). The WHO (2020) advised from the outset that successful approaches to the management of the virus were through local measures, particularly test, track, trace (TTT) and isolate. Those countries that used this approach, based on their experience of SARS (Mason 2012), brought in local teams to check those suspected of being infected and the people that had been in contact with them were isolated. Those isolated were supported by the Government, through finance, food, medical supplies or family support (Beaubien 2020). In stark contrast with this, the initial implementation of TTT by Public Health England (PHE) was closed down on 12 March (Briggs et al 2020), on the basis that the Government did not have adequate capacity at the centre. This was an unusual approach, given that every local authority in the country has TTT capability for managing existing notifiable diseases, sexually transmitted diseases including AIDS (Briggs 2005), and also other outbreaks such as food poisoning and waterborne diseases such as Legionnaire's disease (Kirrage et al 2007). In centralising this approach to TTT, then, the traditional public heath role of local authorities was set aside (Ham 2020).

A second approach to centralising the pandemic was to prioritise the NHS over other forms of social care. While this was understandable in the public's mind initially, not least when there were no effective therapies for managing the virus, it became less acceptable when it was found that hospitals were cleared of older patients, who were transferred to care homes without being tested for the presence of the infection. The NHS has a much greater and unified voice in Government, not least since the head of the NHS (Daly 2020) and the PM were friends at university. Also, the care sector is fragmented, primarily used by older women, and the management of the homes is privatised. Successive governments have failed to deal with the issues of providing adequate funding for social care and, as a result, many care workers are on zero-hours contracts and minimum wage (Cookson 2020). This meant that they were frequently moving between care homes to create liveable incomes (Pegg 2020). Furthermore, the staff in care homes were not provided with PPE despite numerous statements to the contrary by the PM. There was evidence of the same behaviour in the second round of lockdown from September 2020 onwards, although this time the blanket 'do not resuscitate' orders were reviewed with the expectation that these would be returned to individual decisions on a case-by-case basis for patients – nevertheless there was no certainty that this would be so (Berg 2020; Booth 2020).

The third way in which the PM has centralised the management of the pandemic has been to deny the resources to local authorities and local Directors of Public Health to support those in need in their areas and to undertake local TTT. At the outset, local authorities were advised to spend what was necessary to support people through the pandemic, and provided with specific funds to help move the homeless from the streets (Jenrick 2020). However, the funds provided were small and did not reflect this promise. Inadequate food parcels delivered by the Government's private sector contracts meant that local authorities were providing a range of other support systems. The PM also centralised the response through the call for volunteers early on in the pandemic. Local authorities were encouraged to recruit volunteers to a national system and over 750,000 people came forward (Murphy 2020a). However, very few of these volunteers were used and this prevented them being utilised at the local level as they were kept on call though the central system. Gradually, local use of volunteers has been restored.

Where the PM was expected to provide a centralised response was through the provision of PPE. The emergency planning exercise Operation Cygnus in 2016 demonstrated that there would be a need for a range of equipment, machines and logistics to support food supply and equipment (Pegg 2020). The PM's response was to use centralised and privatised procurement from companies that were known to the Conservative Party as donors (NAO 2020e). Hence the PM centralised the management of the pandemic through 'crony' appointments to the leadership of TTT, the vaccine taskforce, and the development of a test track and isolate app. The centralisation of the pandemic has partly been associated with the PM's personalised, presidential style of government, as, by acting alone, it is said that he is able to change direction quickly (Mount 2020a; 2020b).

III: Privatisation

As part of the reinforcement of a centralised approach to managing the pandemic, and one that fitted with the PM's ideology for promoting the private sector to deliver public services (Mount 2020a; Johnson 2020), private contractors were used rather than local government in distinct contrast with the experience of the previous 100 years. This was against the advice of the WHO (2020) and the practices of other countries that were ahead of the UK in managing infection rates (Bienbeau 2020). The emergence of the private sector approach was in the supply of PPE for hospitals and care homes. In October 2019, the Government had decided to stand down its supplies of PPE and it was quickly clear that there were considerable shortages that required close management and reuse of equipment (IPS 2020). The PM's office approached major garment manufactures including Burberry to make and supply PPE, although there was no evidence of any experience of this kind of work. It was reported that Burberry was one of the companies known to the PM's advisers in No 10 (Davies 2020). At the same time, British manufacturers of PPE supplying international markets offered their stocks to the Government via emails, phone calls and their MPs but received no replies.

The privatised approach adopted by the PM not only allowed the pandemic to be under central control but also the Government expenditure for the contracts that were awarded. As the NAO (2020e) found, the methods adopted to procure contracts did not meet the Government's rules. The contractors selected were primarily based on personal recommendations from Conservative Party politicians, and these recommendations placed nominated contractors in a 'fast lane' where they were more likely to be awarded contracts. This explains the media stories of PPE suppliers being appointed without any previous experience (Conn and Lawrence 2020). This approach to appointing nominated suppliers was primarily in the provision of PPE. The contracts that were awarded to

Serco and Deloitte for TTT were from the existing contract framework. However, it appears that the contracts issued had no default clauses for poor performance. There had already been some consideration of their fitness to provide and then both Serco and Deloitte subcontracted the TTT work to other companies without there being any checks on their fitness to deliver, despite them being criticised for failures in delivery. The contract for advice on the NHS 111 number was also examined after it was found that it was 'dangerous' and incorrect, and this contract approach was stopped (Conn 2020).

Another privatised approach was to book nearly all the hospital capacity in the private sector early in the pandemic (Illman 2020). The purpose of these contracts was to enable non-COVID-19 operations to go ahead for cancer and cardiac surgery. In another, smaller contract area, the provision of food for those shielding, the Government paid double the price for each box compared with the value of the contents (Chakelian 2020) – the food in many of the boxes was not nutritious and was the same each week.

A further supply issue was through the provision of ventilators for hospitals' Intensive Care Units (ICUs). Instead of approaching existing UK manufacturers and suppliers of ventilators, the Government instigated a national ventilator challenge to private sector companies. A study undertaken by the NAO (2020b) examined both how the Government procured ventilators and how the Cabinet Office managed the challenge. The study raised the issue of the mechanisms of procurement for ventilators, which were also the subject of a wider procurement report (NAO 2020c). Initially it was assumed that the Government needed to acquire 30,000 ventilators to add to the 7,400 that were already available in the NHS in March 2020.

> However, in the week commencing 13 April, only around 10,900 mechanical ventilator machines were available to the NHS across the whole UK. This

comprised around 9,100 existing units the NHS had by then found it already had access to across the UK, around 1,200 on loan from the private sector, around 400 newly purchased by DHSC and around 200 manufactured through the Cabinet Office ventilator challenge. (NAO 2020b paras 2.9, 2.10)

By the beginning of August 2020, the target for the NHS having access to 30,000 ventilators was reached, with 12,300 ventilators having been built through the Cabinet Office challenge route. The NHS had also acquired nearly 27,700 non-invasive ventilators which were being used more frequently. At no time was this volume of ventilators required and they have been placed into storage. In order to procure these ventilators, the Government exhausted the stocks from suppliers and then went through intermediaries and finally to direct suppliers, primarily from China. The NAO found that this procurement, although supported by DfID and FCDO, did not have the usual checks on quality and compliance and included pre-paid orders and increased purchase prices. The Cabinet Office appointed a technical design authority with speed and design compliance prioritised over cost.

The next area where the Government used the private sector was in TTT. This was initially coordinated by PHE but when the results were poor, the PM decided, on advice from his then adviser, Dominic Cummings, that PHE should be broken up and two new organisations should be formed. The first was to be headed by Baroness Dido Harding without any formal process of appointment. Another organisation, the UK Vaccine Taskforce, was established in April 2020 and immediately headed by Kate Bingham, a friend of the PM's sister, who appointed her own PR company, which has links to Cummings' father-in-law, on undertaking this role. Bingham also has connections with the vaccine companies and is expected to gain £46m from the UK's vaccine purchase (Syal 2020b), information that was withheld from Parliament. She is married to a Conservative MP. She shared secret information to US investors about which vaccines would be on the UK's procurement list (Syal 2020a). The Government's chair of public appointments, Peter Riddell, has expressed his concern about the politicisation of public appointments (Dunton 2020), while the Commissioner for Standards in Public Life has also raised the issue of the changing culture of government in the application of these standards (Evans 2020). The PM's adviser on the conduct of civil servants also resigned on 29 November following the PM's rejection of his report on Ministerial bullying. The performance of TTT continued to be poor (Fraser and Briggs 2020).

The support provided for business was made through three separate initiatives: the Bounce Back Loans scheme that provided loans of £50,000 or 25% of annual company turnover; and the Coronavirus Business Interruption Loan Scheme (CBILS) followed by the Coronavirus Large Business Interruption Loan Scheme (CLBILS), which offer a range of support including loans and bank overdrafts and 'eat out to help out' which may have been associated with a summer COVID-19 spike (Hern 2020). The Bounce Back scheme was launched after businesses complained that the other two schemes were taking too long to access and operated without requiring credit checks on the companies applying for loans. The loans have been made available through commercial lenders and businesses are expected to pay back in full. If they delay, this will affect their credit ratings and the Government has provided a guarantee to lenders if there is a default. The scheme is managed by Department of Business, Energy and industry (DBEIS), the Government's British Business Bank and HM Treasury. However, the DBEIS accounting officer required a Ministerial direction for the establishment of these schemes (NAO 2020a), indicating that they had some aspects that the civil service did not support: 'A ministerial direction is requested when an AO, usually a permanent secretary, believes that a spending proposal breaches any of the following criteria: regularity; propriety; value for money; or feasibility' (NAO 2020a: 6). In this case, a Ministerial direction was required on all four criteria. The British Business Bank raised similar concerns through its procedures. After receiving approval for the scheme by the Chancellor of the Exchequer, the Secretary of State at the DBEIS instructed the Permanent Secretary to proceed.

The NAO has undertaken a review of the scheme and its operation, as it is the largest and most risky support scheme that has been introduced by the Government (NAO 2020a). The NAO estimates that the Government has committed up to £38bn in the period up to 4 November 2020, and that this was substantially more than had been anticipated; by early September 1.2 m loans had been approved with 90% going to very small micro businesses with turnover of less than £66m. The scheme has high costs which are related to its establishment using outsourced methods and processing which required considerable double data entry. There were no checks on duplicate applications by businesses to different lenders. The speed of the system together with the removal of any background checks has meant that the NAO (2020a) has found that the scheme has been left open to significant fraudulent claims, through a significant rise in new company formation. It has been expected that between 35% and 60% of loans may be defaulted, with the Office for Budget Responsibility (OBR) suggesting that these defaults might range between 15% and 78% depending on the bounce back of the economy. There were also concerns from the DBEIS that these were 'deadweight' loans given their lack of targeting (NAO 2020a). The Bounce Back Loans scheme also crowded out banks and lenders outside the largest five, enabling the latter to increase their market share of Small and Medium Enterprise (SME) customers, with the largest providing £31.3 billion of loans under the scheme, while the remaining 18 lenders were responsible for £3.9 billion (NAO 2020a: 41).

IV: Politicisation

The approach taken by the PM in leading the pandemic has also been to politicise it. The PM has done this through the different treatment of Conservative and Labour-led local authorities when they were in the same required local lockdown. In Greater Manchester MCA, where there is a Labour Mayor, Andy Burnham, there was a joint approach across the local authorities and MPs. However, the PM undermined this solidarity by offering Bolton, a Conservative-run local authority within Greater Manchester, a specific deal. In Leicester, the city is led by a former Labour MP as a directly-elected Mayor, and it is also the constituency of the shadow Secretary of State for health. However, when the peripheral areas of Leicester, outside the administrative boundaries of the city and represented by Conservative MPs, complained about this lockdown, they were removed before the Labour-represented areas.

The PM faced a further range of local issues when the second virus spike in September/October appeared. In imposing local lockdowns in northern England, without any seeming medical evidence and no real improvement over time, the PM was criticised by his own MPs, with nearly 100 said to be waiting to vote against the Government. The PM managed to overcome this revolt through promising votes on future measures. Some local authorities started legal actions against the PM while others suggested that the PM had not appreciated that COVID-19 would never be brought under any kind of management without local action and cooperation, and that this would not be achieved by imposition. However, when the three-tier system was introduced in October 2020, there was no vote on the application of the highest restrictions in the Liverpool City Region.

In the long and public negotiations with the Mayors of Greater Manchester and the Liverpool City Region about funding for furlough and businesses required to be closed, the PM stated that there was no additional funding to support them. Three weeks later, on 5 November, the PM introduced a national lockdown in England, which provided enhanced support for those on furlough and some small businesses at the level provided in the first lockdown and at higher levels requested by the two Mayors. In the North, comments were made that this business support funding was only made available when London and the South-East went into lockdown. The approach to provide local funding 'deals' for each of the lockdown areas was a direct change to the traditional approach of reaching funding agreements based on the Belwin and Barnett schemes. This approach was short-lived, as in the third round of tiered English local lockdown, from 2 December, funding was made by population and not negotiated.

The approach to politicising the introduction of lockdown and differences in funding has been a concern to some of the northern Conservative MPs newly elected at the 2019 General Election. In response they have formed a Northern Research Group, modelled on the European Research Group, with the intention of acting as an internal Parliamentary lobby group within the Party. They have been joined by MPs from the East Midlands.

Brexit, COVID-19 and centralisation

The approach of the PM to centralise the management of the pandemic through contracts and contacts has demonstrated a focus on centralisation. It has also created a potential clientelism and a transactional form of government. Yet the PM's actions have been solely for England, and a more traditional approach to managing a pandemic has been taken in the devolved administrations. While not having control over their management of COVID-19, the PM has been exercising his centralising powers through Brexit, and this will be discussed in the next chapter.

THREE

The Role of the Devolved Nations in Meeting COVID-19

Introduction

In the response to the COVID-19 pandemic, all states have taken their own approaches based on their conditions and existing distribution of responsibilities between tiers of government. While the WHO advice from the outset was to manage the pandemic at a local level, with a focus on track, trace and isolate (WHO 2020), the extent to which this has been undertaken, even within more developed countries, has varied (Christensen and Lægreid 2020; Beaubien 2020). Within the UK, the responsibilities for public health are devolved and, while the four countries worked together at the outset in managing the pandemic (Sargeant 2020), this shifted once the PM started to adopt a different approach for England. The JMC was not invoked in the first days of the pandemic and instead the FMs were invited to participate in COBRA meetings (Sargeant 2020), but this arrangement started to disintegrate when the PM decided to move more quickly out of lockdown in England. This differentiated approach has had important effects on the perception of the devolved nations, the strength of their leadership, and the exercise of their autonomy.

The differences in managing the pandemic in the four UK nations has highlighted the reality of devolution in ways that have not been apparent before to those living in England (Cushion et al 2020). The pandemic has given the devolved nations and their leaders a national stage in new ways. During the course of the pandemic, the FMs in Wales and Scotland have become recognised figures across the UK and their actions have provided a stark contrast with those taken by the PM. Many of the initiatives adopted in Scotland and Wales, ahead of England, have been dismissed and belittled by the PM only to be adopted shortly afterwards. These range from the adoption of face coverings to the management of examination results for 16- and 18-year-old school students.

Within the period of the pandemic, the UK was negotiating its post-Brexit trade deal with the EU for when transition ended on 31 December 2020. For the devolved administrations, their Parliaments and Assembly were founded on the powers associated with the implementation of EU directives and regulations within the UK, and these were supplemented by further financial powers for Scotland in 2012 following further EU subsidiarity agreements in 2009 (Pazos-Vidal 2019). Preparation for life outside the EU has also been subject to a range of legislation, particularly on the UK internal market, environment, transport and higher education, which has moved powers away from the devolved administrations and back to Whitehall. This has been depicted as a 'power grab' by those supporting devolution but as a 'power surge' by the PM (Torrance 2020). In this chapter, leadership of the pandemic within the four nations of the UK is discussed; their distinctive approaches and the effects of the heightened recognition of borders within the UK and on the island of Ireland are considered. This is set within the context of devolution and its prospects in a post-Brexit settlement for the nations that is further considered in Chapter Five.

The role of the EU in devolution and its application in the UK

The role of the EU in supporting the practice of devolution within member states, the principles set out in EU treaties (1957, 1992, 2019), and their cumulative application, have generated a framework for devolution within the UK through the principle of subsidiarity (Millar and Scott 1993; Grant 1993; Schutze 2009; Pazos-Vidal 2019). The EU is primarily motivated in promoting devolution as a counter to the charges of a democratic deficit (Kauppi 2018). This is a particular concern for the EC and the exercise of its administrative role (Bekkers et al 2016; Murdoch et al 2018). In part this has been addressed through the expansion of the role and powers of the European Parliament, illustrated through the UK's Brexit process, in holding the final veto on any agreement.

The increase in direct relationships between the EC and subnational government, in ways that are not filtered by member states, has been another mechanism for countering claims of centralisation. The changing role of the Committee of the Regions (CoR) is part of this 'grandparent' relationship between the EC and local and regional governments of member states (Morphet 1994; Loughlin 1996). The CoR was established in 1992 with members primarily drawn from directly-elected regional and city politicians. The UK is an exception to this. Initially, the UK Government decided to appoint civil servants and other nominees to these CoR seats, but eventually they were filled by nominated local government representatives (Pycroft 1995). Following this, it has promoted Multi-Level Governance (MLG) as a key operational principle (CEC 2001; Morphet 2013). MLG has been used to promote integration and subsidiarity (van den Brande 2014; Pazos-Vidal, 2019) through three principles in the EU's treaties: fairness, subsidiarity and cohesion. In the UK, without these treaty principles, there would be no legal pressure to implement devolution although there is strong influence from the OECD (2001; 2020a). It is also through these principles that devolutionary practices are being viewed.

Devolution practices in the UK have been based on subsidiarity, a principle present within the EU from the outset (Wallace 1973). Its role and purpose were accelerated in the Treaty for the EU (TfEU) in 1992 (Wilke and Wallace 1990; Wall 2008). This was initially stimulated by member-state criticism that the EU was becoming too centralised (Pollak 2000), but it was also associated with the accession of the Eastern European states. The expansion of the principle of subsidiarity within the EU as part of the TfEU was first developed in 1988. This gave the UK Government some time to prepare for its application within the UK (Goetz and Mayer-Sahling 2009). However, the UK Government applied subsidiarity within domestic legislation rather than through constitutional change (Trench 1993), allowing for its future removal.

The application of the principle of subsidiarity in the UK was accompanied by specific programmes and policy development in Northern Ireland, Scotland, Wales and London. In Northern Ireland, the principle guaranteed devolved government, was protected through a specific treaty, the Belfast/Good Friday Agreement (GFA) 1998, and provided a more solid foundation for the peace process within the guarantees provided to all parties (Carmichael and Knox 1999; McCrudden 2015). In Scotland, Wales and London, the devolution principles enabled decentralisation of decision making, especially in relation to the operational delivery of specific EU programmes and policies (Borghetto and Franchino, 2010). The matters that were reserved for Whitehall were those that fell outside the UK's pooled decision making within the EU and, with some small exceptions, this boundary has been maintained (Cairney 2006; Aroney 2014). In London, the creation of a new authority for London, with a directly-elected Mayor with decentralised decision-making powers, was a different type of reform. The Greater London Authority (GLA) is legally defined as a local authority. Its creation prefigured the reforms that were eventually proposed for local government in England introduced in 2000, and it gave the Mayor of London significant control over funds and programmes that remain centralised elsewhere in England. While this settlement was described as representing a new devolved state, in practice it extended to operational issues and was a tool of decentralisation. The enhancement of powers for the Scottish Parliament and Welsh Assembly for decision making on operational programmes has increased since 1999, together with some tax-raising powers. The completion of the UK's withdrawal from the EU through Brexit removes these treaty obligations for subsidiarity and gives no long-term assurance for the existence or role of the Scottish and Welsh Parliaments, or Northern Ireland Assemblies.

To promote economic and social success, the EU has found ways to counter the political and operational practices of member states to support investment in specific locations. Variable geometry might have been a pragmatic approach in the short term, as the EU enlarged. However, having no agreed optimal level of devolved decision making to achieve economic plans within the member states has increasingly been seen as detrimental to the EU's longer-term economic vision (Jamet 2011). This may require investment in infrastructure and skills that are not priorities for member states. The EU also wishes to optimise the benefits of the new economic geography (Krugman 1991). The OECD has found that there is a benefit to domestic GDP where sub-state administrative boundaries reflect the Functional Economic/Urban Area (FEA/FUA), and where these sub-regions have strong directly-elected leaders (Ahrend et al 2014). The EU has been working with the OECD to define the optimal FUAs for the EU (Dijkstra and Poelman 2012; OECD 2013) and then, through cohesion policies and programmes, to reinforce this scale through economic, administrative and government units across its territory. The institutional mechanism of Integrated Territorial Investment is an emerging organising principle for this approach (van der Zwet et al 2014; Ferry et al 2018).

The EU provenance of devolution in the UK has meant that it has always been contested and accommodated (Convery 2013). When devolution was introduced, the primary responsibility of the Parliament and Assemblies was the implementation of EU legislation (Torrance 2020). While representatives of the Scottish Parliament at Ministerial and official level have been able to accompany UK Ministers and officials to EU Council meetings on sectoral issues, such as transport, they have no official role and cannot contribute in ways that differ from UK central Government policy (Tatham 2008; McAllister 2000). This instability in the devolution settlement has also been exemplified through the operation of the BIC, which is attended by the First and Prime Ministers of Scotland, Wales, Northern Ireland, Jersey, Guernsey and the Isle of Man and Ireland (Morphet and Clifford 2018). The UK and England were initially represented by the de facto or appointed Deputy Prime Minister but this was then downgraded to the Secretary of State for Northern Ireland. Furthermore, these meetings have no English press coverage. In one of her last acts, at a meeting in Scotland to announce a city deal with Stirling, PM May announced a review of devolution which has terms of reference that confirm and emphasise the role of Whitehall, not of further devolution (May 2019; HMG 2019a; Donoghue 2020). In Convery's (2013) terms, this provides a decisive demonstration of how the Conservative Party has chosen the centre over devolution as its preferred governance model (Dahlström et al 2011; Smith 2011).

Since 1999, this fluid approach to devolution within Whitehall has been considered and described in several ways as dualism (Marsh 2010), unmanaged divergence (McGrattan and Williams 2017), 'permissive autonomy'(Jeffrey 2007), or 'constructive ambiguity' (Sandford and Gormley-Heenan 2020), leaving an 'unchanged centre'(Mullen 2019). However, when UK devolution practices are cast within the wider framework of EU membership, these subsidiarity principles are protected by successive treaties. The fluidity of these relationships matches more closely the cumulative nature of EU legislation (Morphet 2013) rather than the episodic approaches, bound by Parliamentary terms, in the UK. It also represents the unsettled relationship that reflects the UK's own ambiguous relationship with the EU that has been illustrated over time (Wall 2008; Morphet 2013).

The four nations' approach to COVID-19

The development of a common approach to managing COVID-19 was undertaken initially through joint meetings of the Governments of Scotland, Wales and Northern Ireland, together with the UK Government representing England as well as the UK (Sargeant 2020). FMs have been meeting regularly to discuss policies including Brexit. Responsibility for health, including public health, is a devolved matter so there was always an understanding that the nations would be leading on their own approaches, while across all nations, including England, public health had been devolved to local authorities and Directors of Public Health in 2012.

The ways in which devolution has functioned and been enhanced by the COVID-19 pandemic can be discussed through an examination of three issues. The first is the extent to which there has been an outward and visible sign of national leadership: what is best for the nation and how the FMs and PM have expressed this to their populations. The second is to consider the extent of distinctiveness of national policy expressed by the FMs and the PM for England and how these have been viewed within each nation and between nations. The third is to consider the extent to which the role of borders has emerged as part of these national leadership strategies. Finally, there is a consideration of how these factors have all served to reinforce the role, rights and character of the devolved nations in the public consciousness and have surfaced the PM's responsibilities for England, which have been in place since 1999, but have not attracted attention before.

I: Leadership

There has been considerable discussion about the effectiveness of national political leaders in the ways in which different countries have managed the virus. Political leadership qualities required in a pandemic are different from those that are generally recognised and respected. Firstly, leaders have had to have an outward focus to give a sense of security to their populations about their government's understanding of the disease and how it is likely to affect their economy and people. Secondly, leaders have to communicate what actions are being taken and what preparations are being made for the future, when the disease accelerates, and for the management of the major economic consequences that will follow. It is important for leaders to communicate why they are imposing restrictions on personal liberty, freedom of movement, and the need to isolate, if necessary. Compliance with these restrictions has some legal underpinning but is primarily by consent. Compliance was a major consideration in a four-nation approach on household mixing for Christmas 2020, when it was agreed that any failure to adhere to restrictions may set a pattern in subsequent months. A third requirement in communication has been providing some expectation that the approaches being adopted will lead to an improved situation even where the future pattern and intensity of the disease is unknown. There has been some commentary about women leaders being more effective in the leadership than men (Garikipati and Kambhampati 2020; Henley 2020). Some leaders, such as Jacinda Ardern, PM of New Zealand, have adopted a very strong public communication strategy while also applying strict lockdown and quarantine measures (McGuire et al 2020; Wilson 2020). In Germany, while operating within a federal system with distributed responsibilities, Angela Merkel has given strong central leadership about how the country is dealing with the pandemic (Crayne and Medeiros 2020). Both countries have achieved smaller death rates per 100,000 population in comparison with other countries.

While the leaders of some countries took a national approach others, as in Italy, took a regional approach, closing down Lombardy first. This is an easier option where regions are part of national constitutions and their boundaries are familiar to inhabitants (Remuzzi and Remuzzi 2020). Much of the debate at the start of the pandemic was about how modelling and other scientific evidence and advice could be used by national politicians in their decision making, while it was local public services that met the force of the pandemic in dealing with patients and the mechanisms of isolation for those in quarantine. In New Zealand, the Government isolated those in quarantine into state-funded hotels and they were not permitted to leave until the period was completed. This was the initial response in the UK where those returning from infected areas in China were sent home on a special flight and then isolated for a period. This approach to managing the virus from other countries lasted until 12 March 2020, after which TTT was set aside on the basis that the country did not have the capacity to continue this system. Following the subsequent response to the first wave of the pandemic, including critical failures to provide adequate PPE (NAO 2020c; 2020e) or ventilators (NAO 2020b), and higher mortality rates than other European countries (Vaughn 2020), all Presidents of the Medical Colleges together with members of the House of Lords sent an open letter to the UK political leaders in June 2020, making the case that preparation for the next round of the pandemic was critical (Adebowale et al 2020).

From the outset, the FMs of Wales and Scotland took a very direct approach in communicating with the public. The FM of Scotland had daily televised press conferences where she announced any changes in lockdown regulations and her Government's response to the pandemic. At one stage, Nicola Sturgeon took the same approach as the PM of New Zealand in hoping that COVID-19 could be eradicated. However, this has not been possible in practice. At these daily press conferences, the FM of Scotland has been open to press questioning and has always addressed her audience in a way that has explained the difficulties facing her and the Scottish Government about what actions to take. Her daily press briefings have had a significant following from other parts of the UK, including

England. There was some suggestion, just before the second spike of the virus in September 2020, that these daily briefings should no longer be televised, but that position was changed as infections rose and following a public petition (Law 2020). However, despite the failure to achieve eradication, the confidence in the FM has increased over that of the PM during the progress of the disease (Curtice 2020). Like the government leaders in Norway, the level of communication and the collaborative common stance on dealing with the pandemic increased public trust and confidence in what is described as 'meaning making' (Christensen and Lægreid 2020).

In Wales, FM Mark Drakeford took a similar approach to communication with regular press conferences. He also undertook personal self-isolation in his garden shed to protect a vulnerable person in his own household (MacMath 2020). The approaches to managing the pandemic in Wales, like Scotland, were based on earlier and more stringent actions than those for England. This restricted population movement to small areas apart from specified reasons, including medical appointments or work. There were limits on people crossing the border from England, as in Monmouthshire, South Wales, where there was a much lower rate of infection incidence than in neighbouring England. North Wales has close links to Merseyside and that has also been a consideration in managing the FM's approach.

In Northern Ireland, the management of the pandemic has been exacerbated by the failures in the NHS before the pandemic struck. Inevitably there have been comparisons with the approach in the Republic of Ireland, which has a mixed market health service. Leadership in Northern Ireland initially replicated that of the UK Government, with the FM Arlene Foster following the PM. However, over time this changed and became more localised. At the same time, the implications of the application of Brexit on the island of Ireland, the repudiation by the PM of his recently adopted Northern Ireland protocol, likely economic downturn, and the failure of the UK Government to resolve how customs will be managed between

the devolved administrations. Under the Barnett formula this would normally be straightforward, but it was not immediately announced, the reason given being that the nations were each at different points in their lockdown strategies. There was some indication that, in order to obtain funding, nations had to engage in the same lockdown centralised programmes, but this approach did not last for long and guarantees were given to each nation. While this caused considerable political disruption, as the PM stated that there was inadequate funding available to support regions and nations, the implementation of a second lockdown in England on 5 November immediately produced much higher levels of financial support for the economy than had previously been requested by local leaders (Sunak 2020).

II: Devolved distinctiveness

While the three nations have continued to work together, each has taken a different path to managing the pandemic. In part this is related to the understanding of national culture and likely responses. COVID-19 has also spread in different ways across the UK. Although each nation has had its own approach to lockdown, travel, mask wearing and meeting others, there are other issues that have to be considered in order to support compliance. While powers and fines are important, for the most part, compliance is voluntary. Compliance with requests to change behaviour to support risk mitigation is related to the level of risk perceived (Huang et al 2012; Shao et al 2017) and, as studies in the US have demonstrated, is related to the confidence that people have in their political leaders at all scales of government (Shao and Hao 2020). Calvillo et al (2020) suggest that compliance involves the relationship between political ideology and threat perceptions that are created through issue framing by political leadership and the media. For a threat, such as that offered by this pandemic, the politicisation of the issue in the media and by leaders has been very salient in the way in which people perceived the threats to them personally.

Where leaders such as President Trump in the US downplayed its significance, that was reflected in the media, his supporters perceived COVID-19 as less of a threat and felt less vulnerable to it as a consequence. These responses to risk also correlate with demographic characteristics including age, class and ethnicity, although COVID-19 is a new type of societal risk so there is less research on how people may respond.

Leadership in any crisis depends on politicians but also on the interpretation of their messages and requests for action by the media and others with expertise and experience. Hence, during COVID-19, the messages from politicians to the public to change behaviours depended initially on uncritical support from these other channels, although this cannot be expected to last as evidence of the effectiveness of the messages and the supporting systems to deal with the pandemic as it unfolds (Newton 2020). In COVID-19, the support of other tiers of government is also seen to be important, not least as the local approach to disease management has been a central message of the WHO (2020), derived from emerging experience of those countries which have been more successful in containing the virus. In effect all scales of government have needed to work together while managing the local experience of the disease. Christensen and Lægreid (2020) argue that the way in which communities are compliant with the requests of the government to support the management of a pandemic or other disaster is also a means of coproduction.

Leadership of COVID-19 has been highly politicised, not only by opponents criticising the effectiveness of governing party actions, but as a more incorporated or 'priced-in' response to the pandemic – it is assumed that the methods of responding to the pandemic will not take the 'what has worked in the past' approach, but rather one that represents a wider political ideology and patterns of governing. Hence in the UK, the PM's highly privatised, outsourced approach to managing the pandemic (NAO 2020b; 2020d) was aligned with his wider political ideology on other matters such as Brexit. While taking a centralised statist approach, he did not use the existing public sector systems that have been in place for over a hundred years. This state privatisation of the pandemic has also been contradictory in practice. While the central state has been expanded particularly to support the economic consequences, the PM has indicated that he is looking for a new approach to the welfare state similar to that proposed by Beveridge (Timmins 2001) but delivered by the private sector (Johnson 2020).

The approaches in the four nations have been distinctive in other ways. In Scotland, Wales and Northern Ireland, there have been close working arrangements between the Government, the local authorities and medical officers of health. The local procedures for TTT have been more systematic and successful than in England, which has relied on a privatised approach (NAO 2020e). Here, after five days of making no contact with those who have been near someone who has tested positive, the details are passed to the local authority by the national centre and, when they have been found, the details have to be passed back to the centre rather than being managed locally. The private sector implementation of TTT has been low in areas of high infection (Fraser and Briggs 2020).

III: Borders

A further way in which the FMs have taken a different approach to the management of the pandemic has been their attitude to borders, all of which are porous. The existence of borders within the UK is marked by road signs welcoming people into different nations, but they have had little other significance. Thus, the introduction of border closures between the UK nations has served to reinforce the different government regimes for managing COVID-19 and the strength of devolved powers. This has made the borders more apparent in ways that have not been the case for centuries in Great Britain and decades on the island of Ireland. This management of borders has taken different forms in each nation. In Wales, the border with England has been closed twice, with police asked to turn back English visitors. This met with unwelcome comments from English people living on the borders but with positive approval from people in Monmouthshire, which had a very low level of COVID-19. The FM of Wales required the PM to close the border before applying his own powers to do so. In Scotland, the border with England was closed on 20 November as part of wider movement restrictions within Scotland. All four nations agreed a common movement strategy for Christmas 2020, with Northern Ireland giving extra days either side of this period.

The approach in Northern Ireland has been different. Initially it followed what the FM Arlene Foster stated was the science cited in support of English approaches and followed these lockdown measures. However, as Northern Ireland shares a land border with the Republic of Ireland, there were also considerations about cross-border movements and disease spread. There were also opportunities to compare the outcomes of two different approaches to managing the virus at close hand. Furthermore, in the period since the GFA, health care initiatives and facilities have increasingly been developed across the border (Heenan 2009; 2020), and the future of this strategy has remained uncertain as a result of Brexit. The call for a cross-border approach to managing the pandemic was made on 31 March by the President of the Royal College of Surgeons in Ireland and also by the President of Epidemiology and Public Health at the Royal Society of Medicine in London (Pollak 2020). A week later, the Medical Directors of Health for Northern Ireland and the Republic signed a memorandum of understanding on full cooperation across the island of Ireland, including on matters such as procurement of equipment. Subsequent meetings were extended to include the Minister for Northern Ireland in the UK Government. However, this agreement appeared to fall apart on the decision to apply different travel restrictions, leading the FM and

Deputy FM to request a meeting of the BIC to discuss a way forward (Pollak 2020). However, other approaches, such as the use of a common phone app to inform people of their contacts following a positive diagnosis, have subsequently been more successful.

The relationship between COVID-19 and Brexit in the four nations of the UK

COVID-19 has reinforced differences in devolved government in the UK that have been of growing concern to the PM. He has made efforts to create a more unified and common approach, but his slow response to changes in COVID-19 infections and a recognition of WHO (2020) advice for local action including the FMs, has encouraged devolved approaches. While it has not been possible within the devolved settlements for the PM to take any action to require the FMs to take common action with England, there has been some sense of a 'pay-back' for this behaviour in the removal of devolved powers through Brexit.

The visibility of the devolved nations and the PM's position as, in effect, the FM of England, has been increasingly understood during the passage of the pandemic (Cushion et al 2020). At the same time, the preparation for Brexit through specific UK legislation has demonstrated the fragility of the legal position of the devolved administrations, with no powers at all for England. The responses to the pandemic in all four nations of the UK has demonstrated for the first time to people in England the real changes that have been brought about in the UK since 1999. Also there has been surprise that the FMs can prevent travel from England to their nations in the same way that other countries have imposed bans on UK residents without quarantine.

FOUR

Getting to the Local: Managing the Pandemic in Practice

Introduction

At the beginning of the COVID-19 pandemic lockdown in England in March 2020, the Secretary of State for local government advised councils to spend what it would take to manage the crisis and then the Government would compensate them (Sharman 2020). This promise was short-lived (Calkin 2020) and the funding provided was a small amount, particularly in comparison with the scale of task required and the size of the private sector contracts given to the companies such as Serco and Deloitte for TTT and privatised PPE procurement.

In Scotland, the response to the pandemic was always cast as a local approach within a national framework, with medical officers of health being supported by local teams including local authorities for TTT, as well as other measures for well-being, the economy and mental health (Scottish Government 2020a). This approach has been accompanied by local protection levels which are similar to the tiered lockdown in England (Scottish Government 2020b). In Scotland, travel outside the local area has always been included in local protection measures but, on 20 November, the FM set out regulations to stop travel to and from England. In Wales, the Welsh Government, Welsh Local Government Association and Public Health Wales (PHW) have been working together throughout the pandemic, coordinated by PHW, which is also aligning the management of the pandemic with Brexit. The test, trace and protect system in Wales has worked with local authorities and local health boards, using a system for following up local contacts of those who are infected which has been successful in contacting 96% of those identified (Stephens 2020), a much higher rate than in England.

When English local government was reformed in the1880s into its current format, the Government was motivated towards these changes to provide a greater protection for the local management of public health. Earlier reforms led by Chadwick (Hamlin 1998) demonstrated that infectious diseases and viruses were localised in the spread and had to be managed in a local way, starting with cholera in Soho. The leadership of Joseph Chamberlain in Birmingham also was based on the principles that healthy, well-fed households and an educated workforce were essential for local and national economies (Marsh 1994). Local authorities were responsible for public heath until 1948 and this focus lead to their development of public housing after the Addison Act in 1919, the provision of public parks and open spaces from the 1890s, and the use of regulations and building control standards to ensure that other risks such as fire, construction collapse, and employee safety were part of the local community's protection against public health issues. Local authorities also took on the responsibilities for providing drinking water, sanitation, safe energy provision in gas and electricity, and regular health checks through schools and local health centres, such as that created in Peckham and Finsbury in London (Chandler 2013).

More recently, local authorities have been central to the local management of foot and mouth disease (McConnell 2003, flooding (Pitt 2007), promoting campaigns for improving health such as child vaccinations and health screening programmes. In 1978, Birmingham City Council managed the last case of smallpox in the world (Williams 2020). The Government has a specific funding provision that can be used to support councils, the Bellwin scheme introduced in 1989 (Sandford 2015), mirrored by the EU solidarity fund for natural disasters started in 2002. Within local authorities, environmental health officers have responsibilities for inspecting premises to safeguard the public from matters such as food poisoning and personal cosmetic procedures (WHO 2012; Marks et al 2015). Where there are specific outbreaks of food poisoning or for other infectious diseases, it is the environmental health teams that have always managed TTT in their areas in a quiet but rigorous way.

The decision of the PM to remove local authorities from the management of TTT, when COVID-19 started to emerge, was met with disbelief. On 12 March, the national TTT approach established by the Government was ended, the reason given being that there was not adequate capacity for this to be conducted across the country. This was despite the advice of the WHO (2020) and the experience of other countries, such as South Korea, which had started to effectively manage the pandemic (Beaubien 2020), and also without any consideration of the role of local authorities in undertaking this role. This was in line with the growing Whitehall and Westminster practice since 2010 to regard local government as a sector to be managed, rather than as a partner in promoting joint initiatives and policy to support the wellbeing of the community. This was particularly the case in England, as in Scotland, Wales and Northern Ireland reciprocal arrangements and joint working between the devolved Governments and local authorities remained good and had been strengthened since devolution. The devolved approaches included a much greater role for local Directors of public health than in England. The failure of the English Government (Drakeford 2020) to work with local authorities also allowed the opportunistic PHE to regain its lead role on the delivery of public health that it lost to local authorities in 2012. By removing local government from TTT, it was possible for PHE to retake executive control, even though the mechanisms to implement it required new major private sector contracts.

During the pandemic, the PM also introduced other major policy reforms that affected local government. Since 2012, the government had introduced MCAs with directly-elected mayors for FEAs, and these were combined roles with the local authorities within their areas. While similar to the devolved powers that were given to the Mayor of London in 1999, the powers were more circumscribed and varied according to each MCA (Sandford 2019; NAO 2017; NAO 2020e; LGA 2020e). Combined authorities:

> have been introduced into England's already complicated local government arrangements. For combined author-ities to deliver real progress and not just be another 'curiosity of history' like other regional structures before them, they will need to demonstrate in an accountable and transparent way that they are able to drive economic growth, contribute to public sector reform and help to deliver improved outcomes in their areas. (Murphie 2019: 105)

MCAs do not have devolved powers for housing expenditure or EU funds as in London. The PM was Mayor of London 2008–16. In the 2019 Queen's Speech (HMG 2019b), before the start of the pandemic, the PM proposed a 'levelling up' agenda to reflect the need to tackle poverty and economic lagging in parts of the country, particularly those that were formerly Labour Parliamentary seats. A devolution White Paper that would extend the MCAs for an additional number of combined authorities across England was announced but not published. Local authorities were also expected to come together to propose new combined authorities in the inter-vening period before publication, in return for devolution deal funding to be spent on a Government determined package of projects.

The White Paper did not appear in June 2020 as expected but the then Minister gave a very clear speech on the approach that would be taken towards creating MCAs across the whole of England (Clarke 2020). This was of great concern to Conservative county councils that were most threatened by this proposal. While appearing on the Government's website immediately it was given, the speech was removed overnight and never spoken of again. The Government later announced that the Minister was leaving the Government for personal reasons and that the devolution paper was shelved. However, discussions were underway for voluntary local government reform into MCAs between Whitehall and local authorities, and they continued. There appears to be an initial Government objective to have MCAs across the whole of the Northern Powerhouse area led by directly-elected Mayors, and there were advanced discussions with Lancashire and North Yorkshire, both Conservative-led councils. This may have had an influence on the tier-three lockdown discussions in Lancashire in October. While MCAs may appear to be a devolving or decentralising policy, in the creation of larger formal groupings of local authorities with directly-elected Mayors, they also provide the opportunity for greater central Government influence, including through seconded civil servants and Mayors included within the national political system. This increasingly provides the PM with greater influence over population and territory. The OECD (2020a) argues that these larger local authorities with boundaries that are coterminous with FEAs, and directly-elected Mayors who have devolved powers, are beneficial for national GDP growth. The MCAs in England have not been provided with the associated freedoms that can make these contributions, apart from the Mayor of London, who is having them removed by the Government (Pickard 2020).

The second set of reforms were published in the Future of Planning White Paper (MHCLG 2020). These proposed to turn the English planning system from local determination within a national framework to one of centrally allocated local authority targets for market housing, national development management policies and design codes. The imposition of an algorithm to determine the number of new homes to be provided in each local authority area demonstrated that in parts of southern England, for example, there would be considerable increases in development in the constituencies of Conservative

MPs. It was also proposed to introduce a nationally set infra-structure levy to replace locally renegotiated contributions from developers. Thus, in England, local government's trust in the PM was further diminished.

Local authority roles in managing crises

While local authorities have always been responders of last resort within their areas, in the 1980s a series of disasters led to a Government review of their role as part of the planning for civil contingencies. In 1989, the Government started to change the approach from civil defence to one that was more broadly based on emergency planning and, in a second review in 1991, local authorities were expected to implement a local emergency planning approach partly funded from their own resources. As Coles (1998) states, emergency planning would never be high on any local authority's agenda, particularly at a time of budget reductions, and there was a risk that this would not receive the priority required. A further review was under-taken by the incoming Labour Government in 1998, which moved emergency planning into a more integrated arrangement at the local level and between departments and agencies of the state (Paul 1999). However, the 9/11 terrorist attacks in the US shifted the UK approach again, making it more centralised and reducing the focus on the local (O'Brian and Read 2005).

After the terrorist attacks in England, it became clear that one of the major issues was that of inter-agency communications during the disaster. There were concerns about telephone systems working on different wavelengths and networks, and the focus was more on the emergency services than on the local authority role. By 2016, emergency planning had changed its local organisation into local resilience fora in England and Wales and Regional Resilience Partnerships in Scotland. A review undertaken by the Emergency Planning College for the Cabinet Office (Pollock 2017) demonstrated that the same issues were of concern, including interoperability between communication systems, lack of priority for the role of emergency planning, failing to learn lessons from past events, and the critical importance of disaster planning exercises to provide real learning of how the system will operate in the event of another disaster. This was to prove to be a critical issue in the prevention of COVID-19, when a major exercise, Operation Cygnus, was undertaken to simulate a major pandemic in 2016 (Scally et al 2020), although the report on its operation was not made public (Pegg 2020).

A further review of local resilience was undertaken by the Emergency Planning College (Leigh 2019), sponsored by Serco, one of the government's main service contractors. Here there was still a focus on the lack of integration between emergency responders to crises but also an indication that the anticipation of emergency events was not well developed. The focus was on cyber threats but Leigh (2019) also indicated that preparation for emergencies was being undertaken by looking back rather than anticipating the future. In examining previous events, such as the Buncefield oil depot fire in 2006, local fire officers said that they had planned for only one of the 48 oil storage tanks to blow up, while 23 exploded in this fire. This scenario was beyond their imagination in anticipating a worst-case scenario. As with Grenfell and COVID-19, these have been regarded as Black Swans (Aven 2015) – unknown unknowns – but as Leigh (2019) points out, was this really the case? When examining failures in anticipating disasters, organisational culture is found to play an important role, where people are unwilling to go against the current ethos in relation to understanding risks.

In addition to the longstanding role of local authorities in emergency planning and local resilience fora, from 2012, their responsibilities for public heath were restored. This was in response to EU policy (CEC 2007). Leadership and funding were given to individual local authorities who appointed Directors of public health (Marks et al 2015). At the centre of Government, PHE (DoH 2010) was created to provide policy and advice, reporting directly to the Secretary of State, with similar arrangements in Scotland, Wales and Northern Ireland, where the relationships were much closer with local government and the community (Davies and Mackie 2019; Farrell et al 2020). Since 2012, there has also been discussion in England about combining NHS responsibilities within the new MCAs and devolving the budget. This would allow more integration for care of older people and service delivery in ways that have been pioneered in Wigan (Naylor and Wellings 2019). However, this devolved responsibility never materialised to the point where the powers were passed to the MCAs and even in Greater Manchester, where this has been most developed, there remained a strong national direction to the discussions (Lorne et al 2019). The budgets and services kept being reduced and changed, with the NHS in favour of partnership or shared decision making rather than the devolution of power. The NHS may have been concerned about a loss of influence in Whitehall should their responsibilities be localised. The onset of the COVID-19 pandemic in February 2020 gave the NHS and PHE opportunities to wind back this devolution to the centre (Scally et al 2020) and introduce recentralisation of all health services (Alderwick 2020).

What roles did the Government give to English local authorities in managing COVID-19?

While the PM did not give local authorities the responsibility for TTT, they started their own systems where infection levels were high, making good the Government's shortfalls and reaching nearly 100% of all contacts (Halliday and Pidd 2020). By October, PHE was reporting that 100 English local authorities were working in partnership with the national system of finding local contacts (PHE 2020), extended to 200 a month later, but local authorities were not permitted to contact them. In the approaches offered after the second lockdown in England, for immediate testing, local authorities have been included in the delivery design from the outset.

However, there were more concerns about the subsequent incentives to encourage people to isolate as part of this process, particularly where there was no financial support. Whereas the nationally contracted TTT system could ask people to isolate, from the call centre, local authorities were able to visit those contacts at home and identify any support that could be provided to enable them to remain at home for the isolation period. This approach is one that has been successfully used in managing the pandemic in countries such as South Korea (Beaubien 2020). However, local authorities were not encouraged or supported to do this.

Local authorities had responsibilities for some of their own care homes or residents they funded in private care homes. This immediately brought them into the management of shortages of PPE and the realisation that infections were being spread through patients discharged into care homes by the NHS but also infected by those care workers on zero-hours contracts who had more than one job, spreading the infection between homes (Ladhani et al 2020). There was also a shortage of care home staff as many who had come to the UK under free movement provisions in the EU returned home when faced with the uncertain prospects of Brexit. The threat of the pandemic in care homes was recognised early in the first lockdown (Iacobucci 2020).

While not ascribing health roles to English local government in managing the pandemic, unlike Scotland and Wales, local authorities were to administer local business grants and to prepare business recovery plans for their local economies. By 21 June, local authorities in England had made 844,434 Coronavirus business payments (LGA 2020c). English councils were also required and funded to move homeless people off the streets and place them in hotels and, by 18 April, 90% of rough sleepers had been offered accomodation (LGA 2020c).

Meanwhile, local authorities were required to keep their other services running. When the national lockdown was implemented on 24 March, advice was issued to local authorities by the Local Government Association (LGA 2020a) on maintaining electoral and democratic processes, although suspending local and Parliamentary by-elections. The advice reminded councils that they are first responders within the Civil Contingencies Act 2004 and their role within the Local Resilience Forum (LRF). Ward councillors were identified as having a specific set of roles including:

- acting as a bridge between councils and communities;
- amplifying consistent messaging through disseminating council and Government information;
- identifying local vulnerabilities, particularly local residents, but also businesses, and feeding this intelligence back into councils;
- working with local voluntary sector groups to provide support and advice for local communities;
- providing reassurance and facilitating support for local residents.

(LGA 2020a: 4)

This guidance also suggested to councils that they should consider setting up arrangements similar to those in previous emergencies for a senior councillor to be a point of contact and to ensure that councils were fully briefed on local circumstances. Councillors were to remain in contact with their MPs. In two tier areas of local government, where the Director of Public Health is employed by the county council, specific communication measures were to be established. The need for consistent and verified communication from all outlets, including personal social media accounts, was also stressed to ensure that unverifiable messages were not being transmitted. Support for councillors in these groups has been provided through networked groups established by the LGA

(LGA 2020b). Of the funding that has been provided by the Government to local authorities, 40% has been used to support adult care services (LGA 2020c). In Hertfordshire, this has in particular been through providing support for care providers, including advice and the supply of PPE, and in Warwickshire by pooling the procurement of PPE for adult care providers (LGA 2020c).

A strong role for local councils was identified in community mapping of support, identifying individuals in need of specific support and providing reassurance. Following this LGA guidance, a range of local actions and arrangements were developed and implemented in addition to LRFs, including Strategic Coordination Groups (SCGs) and Local Outbreak Control Boards (LOCBs), to manage information and communication and provide oversight for local TTT and containment systems (LGA 2020b). Each LOCB was required to prepare a Local Outbreak Control Plan within guidance provided by the Association of Directors of Public Health (ADPH 2020) drawn together with PHE, the Faculty of Public Health and the LGA, among others. This approach stressed a multi-agency approach at the local level but did not include any commitment by government to integrate TTT systems that were operating at the national level.

What did English councils do in addition to Government assigned roles?

In addition to these responsibilities, English local authorities undertook a range of initiatives to support their communities during the first lockdown and subsequently. Some, such as Leeds, supported food delivery to vulnerable residents, and others, such as East Suffolk, provided a fund to support community organisations continuing their supporting roles (LGA 2020c). A number of councils also worked to support local businesses. In addition to the distribution of Government business support funding, the Wirral Council provided some of their own funding and worked with the local chamber of commerce to provide business support advice (LGA 2020c). Others, like Elmbridge, particularly focused their support on the high street (LGA 2020c). Some councils, such as Kingston upon Thames, have focused on support for mental health (LGA 2020c), and others on the reopening of parks to provide an opportunity to support physical and mental well-being. Councils have also experienced a considerable increase in the use of online library services through the issue of e-books and talking books (BBC 2020).

In addition to the support services for communities and individuals, local authorities have been maintaining their other functions. These include activities such as determining planning applications. The construction industry had one of the shortest lockdown periods of any sector and local authorities quickly adapted to holding online meetings to consider planning applications where necessary. Local authorities requested and received changes in the planning legislation to allow planning committee meetings to comprise both virtual and physically present attendees (LGA 2020e), and established a case-study hub that provided shared experience and learning for all English councils (LGA 2020c). The Planning Inspectorate also amended their processes so that evidence could be given under oath on enforcement cases online and that planning appeals and examinations could be undertaken virtually, and similar changes in procedure were introduced by the Chief Planner in Scotland.

In Wales, the Government issued specific guidance about placemaking and recovery after the pandemic (Welsh Government 2020), while in England advice was issued by the LGA (2020b) through proposing a range of specific activities:

- shaping and agreeing recovery strategies;
- leading and representing;
- supporting individuals;
- embedding community resilience;

- supporting community cohesion;
- scrutiny and lessons learnt;
- strengthening the council;
- maintaining wellbeing.

(LGA 2020b: 4)

The first of these responsibilities, shaping recovery strategies, was a reinforcement of the local leadership role that was strongly identified in the 1997 Local Government White Paper and the Local Government Act 2000. In order to lead this social recovery, councils were asked to prepare a strategy and implementation plan with the partners. In some two-tier areas of local government, such as in Suffolk, this approach was led by the county council. As with the approaches to developing Sustainable Community Strategies in the Local Government Act 2000, the recovery strategies focused on the economic, social, community and environmental wellbeing of their areas. There was also an approach to considering the organisational changes required to support these enhanced recovery roles. In June, there was an expectation that this would be the main focus on the following six-month period to the end of the year (LGA 2020c). However, in practice the second half of 2020 has been focused on support for local communities and businesses through changing regulations, guidance and partial local lockdowns.

In its report, *Rethinking local*, the LGA (2020c) expected local government to make its case for leading localities out of the pandemic, rather than relying on central Government initiatives. The tone of this report suggests that local government was using this approach to reset central-local relationships (Rhodes 2018) and seize back the initiative away from increasing centralisation since 2010. It located this position in the expectation of the Devolution White Paper aligned with the Chancellor's Spending Review, that was to be published in June 2020 before being postponed. In this devolved role, local authorities were seen as the mechanisms for ensuing that central Government departments were brought together to work at the local level in the same kind of role as local strategic partnerships from 2000–2010. Local government was anticipating powers and funding to change its role in the state to one of local leadership, as a return to the Local Government Act 2000 and away from the centralisation of the Localism Act 2011. This did not happen in the 2020 Spending Review, where additional funding for local projects was centralised (Sunak 2020).

Local lockdowns

While the PM's decision to largely exclude local government in managing the pandemic at the local level and replace them with private sector contractors was unexpected, given the contribution of local authorities in past public health crises, the implementation of local lockdowns was even more baffling. As the PM had not defined a role for local authorities in England for TTT, local authorities devised their own local initiatives, based on ADPH guidance (ADPH 2020), although without central Government funding. This meant that they had little control over understanding the local hotspots from the TTT data that was being published at national level but not provided in detail to local Directors of public health or GPs. Councils were provided with some funds to provide support to vulnerable adults and facilities for those in need of family support or food, but this was not adequate. Increasingly, poorer families were becoming reliant on foodbanks and the national debate, led by the footballer Marcus Rashford, concerning the provision of free school meals for children during school holidays, ran out of steam when the Government's claim that funding had been provided for the October half-term proved not to be the case. The Government relented and announced funding.

When the PM introduced the first round of local lockdown measures in Luton and Leicester, there was no additional local support provided for councils, individuals or businesses at the outset. These lockdowns were imposed without any indication of conditions which had to be met to remove them from local lockdown. The imposition of these lockdowns did not appear to be supported by evidence of how they would work. After lobbying, the PM removed the Conservative areas from lockdown first, illustrating a trend in England of areas with Conservative councils that were subject to fewer lockdowns than Labour areas. This included the PM's own constituency of Hillingdon, which was shown to have a higher infection rate than areas that were in lockdown. At the end of the second national lockdown period on 2 December, Leicester remained in lockdown, still demonstrating a high number of cases and with no indication of what support was likely to be given to change this position.

The second phase of local lockdowns was in larger areas, predominantly in the North-West of England, Yorkshire and Humberside. In this phase, the lockdowns were 'negotiated' between the PM and the local authority leaders, including directly-elected mayors of the MCAs. It is interesting to note the introduction of negotiation into these lockdowns after the enforced approaches in Luton, Leicester and Liverpool, and it was unclear why the Government moved to this position after taking specific powers for imposed local lockdowns previously. The position in Greater Manchester was said to be compounded by the responsibilities of the MCA's Mayor for some health functions and as the Crime Commissioner, with responsibilities for the police, and it was said that if the Government had taken over and the Mayor disagreed that this would cause concern about lines of police accountability. The second reason may have been the strong support of local Conservative MPs for the Mayor's stand – including that of Sir Graham Brady, chair of the Conservative MPs' backbench 1922 Committee. In early October, Sir Graham had already led a backbench rebellion against the Government through the Brady amendment, which sought to have Parliamentary discussion and approval for local lockdowns. The PM agreed with his MPs that national lockdowns would be brought to Parliament but, nevertheless, Sir Graham had made his views clearly known on the efficacy of the lockdown and the support required for local communities and businesses. Sir Graham's role as chair of the 1922 Committee was also important as he is responsible for taking any votes of no confidence in the PM's leadership.

Another reason for a negotiated rather than imposed local lockdown approach could be the powers held by the PM. While it can be argued that any local lockdown needs the consent of local political leaders, including councillors and MPs, it is also the case that, until the end of 2020, when the UK left the EU, the principles of subsidiarity still applied and, as such, prohibited governments taking any action or expenditure that are best undertaken at levels below the state. The WHO (2020) has advised that local lockdowns and management of the pandemic, including TTT and isolate are more effective. While it might be considered that the Government would not wish to be bound by these principles, the threat of legal proceedings against the Government for their action in Greater Manchester and elsewhere may have used this argument. This would not have been welcomed by the Government.

The PM's proposed local lockdown in parts of Greater Manchester included curfews for bars and restaurants, and no compensation was proposed above the national schemes. The directly-elected Mayors of Liverpool, Manchester, South Yorkshire and West Midlands all requested additional support to assist in encouraging compliance. There was a growing sense of weariness with the lockdown and also, despite implementing these lockdown measures over a period of weeks, the infection rates continued to grow. Here the negotiations for greater local lockdowns were public and fraught. The PM finally resorted to imposition in the Liverpool City Region rather than negotiation. In Greater Manchester, the negotiations continued with strong support from all the local authorities and MPs, including Conservatives, until the PM imposed lockdown, initially stating that Greater Manchester would not receive the same level of support funding as the Liverpool City Region and Lancashire. This appeared to be the PM applying a direct sanction for the local public campaign waged by Mayor Burnham. The PM gave in and provided support almost to the level that Burnham had requested. However, this support was also not initially extended to the devolved administrations, bringing further criticism about the politicisation of local support, although this was also overturned. Three weeks after this incident, the PM imposed the second national lockdown, complete with a financial support package that had been requested by Mayor Burnham. This brought immediate criticism of the PM only responding to business and local needs when London and the South-East were brought into lockdown, and leaving the PM's manifesto commitment of 'levelling up' the country in tatters.

The third round of local lockdowns in England was introduced at the end of the second period of national lock-down on 2 December. This round operated a similar tiering approach as in the second local lockdown, but with no local negotiation. Here the criteria of lockdown, funding support, and expecting associated local mass testing were part of the PM's lockdown plan (HMG 2020). In this approach, proposed to Parliament for acceptance, it was expected that each locality would be examined every two weeks with a view to changing their tiered status. There were no local negotiations and all areas were to operate within one of the three designated tiers. The PM initially intended this third local lockdown period to last until the beginning of April 2021, but reduced this period following opposition from his MPs. However, this approach was not supported by over 70 Conservative backbench MPs in the COVID Recovery Group (CRG), who wrote to the PM on 22 November requesting evidence of why this approach would work, without which they would vote against the proposals. The number of Conservative MPs supporting this letter is significant as the PM's majority in Parliament is 80 and it is only his own MPs, through the mechanism of the 1922

Committee of backbench MPs, that can force him to resign. Hence, in the third local lockdown period, local authorities had no influence over a centrally-imposed system, but MPs used their powers in Parliament to argue for local rather than national measures. This new-found localism in Parliament has also been supported through the creation of other territorial interest groups, including the Northern Research Group, which has extended to include MPs from the East Midlands. With the presence of Scottish National Party MPs in Parliament and regional and local groups of MPs, Parliament is beginning to reflect increasingly local interests and sub-national affiliations responding to the centralising actions that have become more apparent through the period of the pandemic.

Has this changed the centre's view of local government?

Despite the level of flexibility and responsiveness to meeting the pandemic at the local level, the PM has continued to reinforce his preference for the role of the private sector over the public sector in the direct delivery of services (Johnson 2020). In the negotiations over local lockdowns, local authorities have been cast as the enemy of the central state in England and holding the government 'hostage'. However, as with the nations, the PM's attempts at increased centralisation through his management of the pandemic has backfired. Instead, consciousness of local power and interests have come to the fore at all levels of the state.

FIVE

COVID-19 and a UK Unitary State Post-Brexit?

Introduction

The moves that have been made by PMs May and Johnson since 2016 to use Brexit and then COVID-19 to 'restore the centre' (Dahlström et al 2011) have been seen at different state scales. The pandemic has both provided opportunities for accelerated centralisation, ahead of Brexit, and for more clearly defining the role of devolution in Scotland, Wales and Northern Ireland. Devolved leadership has become more distinctive and has increased trust in the devolved Governments over that for the PM (Curtice 2020). The position in England has also been made more transparent as a consequence. Despite the PM starting the pandemic with a UK approach, very rapidly he has been shown to be the FM of England. The longstanding confusion of UK Ministers not knowing when they are speaking for the UK or for England has had to be addressed (Cushion et al 2020). The differences between the independence and local determination in the three nations in comparison with England has not only led to greater regional and local identification and leadership in England from local government and Mayors of MCAs, but has also been reinforced by MPs. At the introduction of the tiered system in England after the second lockdown from 2 December, MPs have strongly argued against national approaches and in favour of local determination of the management of the pandemic at individual local authority level.

The effect of the pandemic in reinforcing confidence in devolution has led to the PM telling his MPs that devolution has been a 'disaster' and the greatest policy failing of PM Blair's time in office. The 2019 Queen's Speech reinforced the role of the Dunlop review of capability in the union established by PM May in July 2019 and appears to have taken a confrontational and competitive approach to working with the devolved administrations (Sargeant 2020). While there has been criticism of four different approaches within the UK for managing the pandemic, efforts to come together to determine a common approach for Christmas 2020 were undermined by the PM's failure to attend the meeting with the FMs, which was noted and criticised by the FM of Wales. Mount (2020a; 2020b) argues that this approach to devolution has been longstanding in the Conservative Party, with Pittock (1998) suggesting that it lies in the roots of Tory philosophy since the 18th century.

The PM's stated wish to reinforce the Union by taking the opportunity of Brexit to remove the powers of the devolved administrations is evidenced through the UK Single Market Act and Whitehall's project-by-project control over the 'levelling up' funds in the whole of the UK (Sunak 2020). However, the PM has not proposed an alternative approach of how a reinforced Union could be created and managed within the UK. Through a collision in the removal of the subsidiarity principle in the UK as a result of Brexit and the COVID-19 pandemic, support for devolution is being strengthened. What alternative scenarios for the future of the UK can be considered after Brexit? While the PM may wish to reinforce the Union through increased centralisation, what other approaches will emerge? These are discussed further on.

The UK as a centralised Union?

The preparation for the implementation of post-Brexit institutions through legislation is demonstrating that the Government is seeking to hold more power in the centre in a range of ways. In the PM's 2019 manifesto and the

Queen's Speech (HMG 2019b), there were commitments to reduce the power and influence of the institutions of the UK Government, including the judiciary and Parliament. In the PM's Government since 2019, the role of the Cabinet has been reduced and there has been increased control from the PM and his office. In the period when Cummings was the PM's lead adviser, he was said to wield more power than any Minister, and the decision to break international law in the UK Single Market Bill (O'Carroll 2020) was rumoured to have been undertaken at the behest of a special adviser, not an elected politician, and caused the Government's chief law officer to resign (Payne et al 2020). The PM is also seeking to have absolute power and to remove any powers of independence for regulatory bodies. After Brexit, while powers of scrutiny over activities such as UK animal welfare and food standards have been given to Parliament in proposed legislation, these are far less than those available within the EU (Rutter 2020). This position has raised concerns about the strength of these safeguards, and the issue of centralising power has also emerged in the proposed establishment of the Office of Environmental Protection (OEP). While indicating that the OEP will be independent, the appointment of the chair and board members will be by the Government and, in an amendment to the Bill going though Parliament, the Government has proposed its own amendment that will allow it to advise the OEP on how to regulate. The OEP was expected to be on the same independent basis as the OBR, established in 2010, where there are Parliamentary powers on the appointment and removal of its head (Rutter 2020).

The Conservative Manifesto 2019 committed to reviewing a wide range of institutions and constitutional elements, including the Fixed-term Parliaments Act 2011 and the Human Rights Act 1998. Since then there has also been the introduction of the review of administrative law, that is used for Judicial Review (JR), and the expectation of a review of the relative rights and responsibilities of the courts, Parliament and the Government. This is seen as a response to the ruling of the Supreme Court finding against the PM's prorogation of Parliament and the number of JR cases being brought on immigration and asylum cases. Lord Dunlop, a former Government Minister, has argued that it is appropriate as the UK's membership of the EU fettered Parliament's freedoms to make legislation on those areas of policy where the UK had pooled sovereignty. On the other hand, Dunlop, who leads the Union capability review (HMG 2019a), was not supportive of a move to a federal structure, as proposed by the Constitutional Reform Group, that would safeguard devolution in Scotland, Wales and Northern Ireland after Brexit. Issues such as the voting system and reform of the House of Lords that have been discussed in the period since 2010 are unlikely to be reconsidered (Anderson 2020).

Other parts of Government operations structures are being reformed through actions. These include the reforms at the centre of Government and to the civil service. These changes have been implemented, in part, through the removal or resignation of permanent secretaries in Government departments, including the Cabinet Secretary, the Home Office, the FCO, and the incorporation of the DfID into the FCDO. These centralising changes have been acrimonious and represent changing power relationships between politicians and officials. This was reinforced by the PM's refusal to accept the report on bullying by the Home Secretary, Priti Patel, which lead to another resignation (Murphy 2020b).

Instead of the civil service and local authorities working together to manage the pandemic, tools of centralised control have been used, including privatised delivery through the use of Conservative Party donor suppliers (NAO 2020f) and personal friends of the Secretary of State for health (Conn and Lawrence 2020), and 'cronyism' through the appointment of Conservative Party members to run Government bodies without any open competition (Batchelor 2020). In the DHSC, for example, PHE, under the direct control of the Secretary of State, has been blamed for poor performance of the TTT system in COVID-19. The PM appointed a Conservative Party Member of the House of Lords and wife of a Conservative MP to be in charge of the system. The same approach has been used to appoint the Chair of the Joint Biosecurity Centre, who is also the wife of a Conservative MP and has been accused of leaking sensitive Government information on procurements to a feepaying US event which provided information on the UK Government's likely investment in vaccines (Syal 2020a). The Government has been issued with legal proceedings over these appointments by the Runnymede Trust and the Good Law Project (4 November, 2020), and the Commissioner for Standards in Public Life and the Commissioner for Public Appointments have both spoken about their concerns about failure to uphold standards (Evans 2020; Dunton 2020).

The Government has also proposed future changes in the civil service (Gove 2020). In a speech at Ditchley Park, Michael Gove, who is responsible for the Cabinet Office, set out their views. Gove characterised, using the words of Gramsci, the centre of Government as being in a transition phase from the old order and what is new, and the crisis was about this. In the 1930s, Gove argues, there was an ideological shift away from Edwardian paternalism and towards the welfare state. He goes on to argue that the country is now in another paradigm shift towards a market state where longer-term practices and public values are interpreted and delivered in different ways (The Economist 2020). This was reinforced by the PM in his speech to the Conservative Party's annual conference (Johnson 2020). Gove argues that the ideological turning point away from the welfare state came in 2008 with the financial crash, a view reinforced by the Chancellor 2010–2016, George Osborne (Osborne 2014). However, it is possible to see a much longer anti-state ideology growing in the Conservative Party since the 1970s, which has run in parallel with the intro-duction of international public sector market liberalisation (Morphet 2021a). Rather than working with partners in the public sector, Johnson's model is more presidential, with the PM and his team in 10 Downing Street working directly to deliver to the people and removing the checks and balances in the British constitution, that is Parliament, the Cabinet, the judiciary and independent regulators. If the PM cannot pull the levers of power in office then, Johnson and Gove argue, it is time to remove them.

The civil service is considered to be the glue that keeps the current system operating, and this is why it is being targeted through these reforms. The onset of the COVID-19 pandemic has hastened the PM's resolve to make these changes, as civil servants are blamed for standing in the way of awarding contracts by seeking ministerial directions (NAO 2020a), the courts can be used to investigate decision making on appointments without due process, and Parliament becomes increasingly sidelined as a nuisance. In these arguments, Gove and Johnson take the position that, rather than the defenders of the public good, the civil service and judiciary do not echo the priorities of the people and stand in the way of their delivery.

The UK's membership of the EU was a means of not only establishing public value in government (Morphet 2021b), but also providing the legal mechanisms to hold the member state governments to account through the European Court of Justice (ECJ). This is at the heart of this centralising reform project: action without accountability other than through the ballot box. Johnson and Gove have been promoting this approach as similar to Roosevelt's New Deal in the 1930s, when the US economy was supported through investment in public works. The approaches being offered this time have had to become secondary to the funding required to keep the economy supported, while the pronouncements about investment have been short-lived. While Maddox (2020) argues that much of the Government's diagnosis of what is wrong with the civil service is true, any reform of the civil service as part of wider constitutional reforms needs to be set within a context of what government is there to do. However, as all

PMs find when they take office, the role of No 10 is not as powerful as they expect. This was discovered by Tony Blair in 1997 when he introduced committees to promote joined-up government by removing departmental silos and focusing on problem solving for places and people (Morphet 2007). In the EU, this has also been recognised as an issue, and the EC has been moving more towards a territorial approach to integrated policymaking and away from specific commissions (Zimakov and Popov 2020).

The structure of the UK Government is similar to the position of local authorities before 2000, where the chairs of committees were primus inter pares within the council, as the PM is in the Cabinet. This was changed after 2000, when each council adopted a constitution that could set out the powers of their executive, whether a directly-elected mayor or a majority party system (Morphet 2007). This was accompanied by changes in council officer structures, where the local authority chief executive became one of the designated officers to be appointed in every council alongside the finance and monitoring officer. Maddox (2020) suggests a similar reform in the Government by strengthening the powers of the Cabinet Secretary over all other departments, although this would be strongly resisted by permanent secretaries (Rhodes 2018), not least as this would remove their direct accountability to Parliament, including for the agencies and sectors that departments may be responsible for, such as local government and train operators.

Since the Fulton Report (HMG 1968) the issue in the civil service has been about skills. Subsequently, agencification and increased use of contractors and consultants to deliver services has reduced the civil service's experience in running activities that interact directly with citizens and businesses. Furthermore, in other EU countries civil servants are educated as lawyers and accountants first (Page 1991), and these skills are the basis of their work. In the British civil service, accountants and lawyers are regarded as advisers to permanent secretaries rather than core skills. As Maddox (2020) indicates, when the pandemic started, the departments did not have enough skills in-house and were dependent on their existing contractors and consultants.

How will devolution fare in this increasingly centralised state? Given the proposed increase in powers and decision making in Whitehall, the powers of the devolved administrations could be expected to dwindle. At the height of their powers, the devolved administrations have been regarded as large county councils by some in Whitehall. The way in which these changes are undertaken could have an effect on how they are received. If the powers of the devolved administrations are reduced rapidly in a confrontational, competitive way, then this could increase the support for independence (Sargeant 2020). If the changes are made more slowly and in an apparently more collaborative way, then the reduction in powers may be more difficult to track and be less of a target for those parties opposing them.

The UK status quo?

While there appears to be considerable pressure for change in the structure of the UK state, once the pandemic is brought under control with vaccines, then the greatest challenge remains the economy (OBR 2020). The PM's majority in Parliament and the confidence expressed in the FMs' management of the crisis might be overwhelmed by the twin effects of COVID-19 and Brexit to suggest that the UK needs to focus on its economic recovery more than any other changes. The elections for the Scottish Parliament in 2021 may represent the high point of pro-independence support, and then the longer-standing concerns about the ability of the Scottish economy to be independent may return. While the position of the UK economy differs from that in 2014, at the time of the last independence referendum in Scotland, in terms of borrowing and debt the economic position may be so overwhelming that there is a call for all parts of the UK to work together for the good of the country. The same sentiments may be reinforced in Wales and Northern Ireland, where the effects of Brexit may be more severe.

However, devolution will not be operating within the status quo ante as, post-Brexit, powers of the Parliaments and Assembly have been reduced. Funding decisions will be made in London for city/growth deals and through the levelling up fund (Sunak 2020). The use of the Sewel Convention may fall into further disuse. In a less dramatic outcome after Brexit, the agreements between the EU and the UK may have fewer differences and again reinforce the arguments to stay the same. If the PM delivers the 'power surge' (Torrance 2020) promised, those arguing for independence may find that there are fewer grounds to support their position and so the tide of support diminishes. This may also be reinforced if the constitutional and inter-Parliamentary arrangements between the devolved nations and England are reformed and put onto a legal basis. This would mean providing a legal basis for the JMC and the Sewel Convention (Arnott 2020), a revolving Chair, (Clifford and Morphet 2015) and a dispute resolution system (McEwen et al 2020). It would also require changed constitutional arrangements for England (Russell and Sheldon 2018) and a Council of Ministers for all FMs, including England on a equal basis, as in the EU (Jenkin 2020). Jenkin (2020) also proposes an intra-Parliamentary Assembly for joint decision making across the UK.

The UK as a federal state?

If there is further pressure for independence, including a referendum in Scotland that appears likely to be successful, then the UK Government may consider a different strategy. As an alternative to independence, the UK Government could offer to move the constitution to a federal structure. This would involve changing the role of the House of Lords into a second chamber that represents the territories of the UK and has a formal role in decision making, as in other countries. The federal structure would have the benefit of maintaining the Union, albeit within a different constitution (Melding 2007), which would identify which powers should be retained at each level and how taxation and other Government funding might be collected and used. Decisions will be needed first about the UK entering into a federation of nations and then subsequently agreed by all four nations (Paun et al 2019).

A federal constitution has a number of supporters in the UK. Former PM Gordon Brown argues that the pandemic and the PM's approach to local lockdowns has demonstrated, through directly-elected Mayors and MPs, that devolution is now a UK issue. Brown (2020) proposes for the House of Lords to become a Senate of the Nations and Regions, and for a constitutional convention to agree a settlement of the future of the UK. This view of a federal UK has also been proposed by Sir Malcolm Rifkind, who was Foreign Secretary in Thatcher's Government 1986–1990. Rifkind argues (Settle 2020) that the devolved settlement is now out of date – the UK is a Kingdom of four nations and the pandemic has led to this being recognised in London. The federal option, which is also supported by the Labour (Ashford 2020) and Liberal Democrat (Chamberlain 2020) Parties, should be put to the UK if there is another independence referendum in Scotland. As it has never been put before, Rifkind considers that it has a good chance of success.

One of the key concerns about the establishment of a federation in the UK is the size and dominance of England through its population and economy, and within England the same issue arises with a concern about the dominance of the South-East. There could be ways of dealing with decision making between two chambers in Parliament as in other countries, such as the US, established as a response to leaving the British system, and in Germany, established by the British after 1945. Another approach is to consider England as four areas of equal size in geography rather than population. This approach has been proposed by the Kerslake UK2070 Commission and the RSA (2021), which have proposed the division of England into the North, the Midlands, the South-East and the South-West. This would leave the South-East dominant in its economy and population size but would narrow the size gap with the other three areas. The four areas would also have coastal, city and rural areas, making them more similar to each other and the other three nations. Each of the four parts of England could have assemblies and devolved decision-making powers.

The UK as an idea?

If any of the UK nations resolved to become independent, without the remaining nations entering into a federation, this could trigger further change. The GFA includes the principle of a referendum for a united island of Ireland, and ways in which this could be implemented are now being considered (Constitution Unit 2020). If Scotland left the Union, the UK could remain, but if there were further departures then this might be resolved by the UK remaining as an idea like the Benelux countries, or having an organisation like the Nordic Council in Scandinavia. This arrangement might have some agreements about borders and other common issues but these would be between independent states. If some of the parts of a former UK decided to join the EU, then there would be the possibility of creating a European Grouping of Territorial Cooperation which would support a range of agreements for cross-border working (Clifford and Morphet 2015).

England's future: unfinished business?

A major consideration in all the discussions about the future of the UK is whether England is a remainder from other changes or is a determinant of what will happen in the future. As the UK has grown, Wales, Scotland and Ireland have become part of an English organisation, although Scotland retained its own legal, educational, and educational system when two sovereign countries came together in the Treaty of Union 1707. As we have seen in the case of Brexit, treaties are not binding in perpetuity.

One of the major concerns is that there has been little or no interest in devolution to an English Parliament since 1999, nor in regional devolution in 2004 (Rallings and Thrasher 2006; Shaw and Robinson 2007). However, COVID-19 has changed some of this thinking. At the outset of the pandemic, the UK Government was continuing to confuse its responsibilities for England and the UK and this was reflected in the media, despite the major broadcast channels providing networked rather than regionally focused services in their main news output (Cushion et al 2020). This was also confusing for the public who did not live in England, so that gradually over the period March to November 2020, the media and Ministers started to be much clearer about the difference between the rules for four administrations, when and how they are set. This has been a major eye-opener for many people in England who have not appreciated the differences in powers and approaches between the four administrations. It has led to the PM being called the FM of England by the FM of Wales.

This recognition of distinctive difference between England, without a separate government or decision-making assembly, and the other devolved nations, could provide an opportunity for England to consider its position (Denham 2020b). Since the introduction of devolution in the UK in 1999, Whitehall has not introduced constitutional reform. At the outset, it was argued that the informal relationships between England and the devolved administrations could be managed through the Labour Party (Laffin and Shaw 2007), and the JMC was not established on a formal and regular basis. Since 2010, these loose arrangements have been demonstrated as inadequate, not least in the successive ruptures of the Scottish independence referendum in 2014, the Brexit referendum in 2016, and

COVID-19 in 2020. Communications have remained poor between the nations and have been strongly criticised by the FM of Wales. Russell and Sheldon (2018) have proposed that this could be improved through putting the JMC on a firmer footing, rotating Chairs and meeting locations, and establishing sectoral fora. This approach has already been adopted by the BIC (Clifford and Morphet 2015; Morphet and Clifford 2018).

While the pandemic may not result in a call for an English Parliament, it has highlighted the leadership, role and powers of the Mayors of MCAs and the way in which they have been treated by the PM. While the devolved administrations have been seen as little more than county councils by Whitehall, there has been a distinct difference between their powers and those of the MCAs. The local lockdown 'negotiations' that took place before the second national lockdown in England were played out in real time in the media. The proposal by the PM to introduce a further period of tiered lockdown across England from 3 December 2020 has also stimulated widespread opposition from approximately 100 Conservative backbench MPs, who are arguing for a locally-determined approach to recovery based on individual local authorities through their CRG.

The future of the UK?

The UK Government's approach to Brexit is one of 'taking back control' (Sandford and Gormley-Heenan 2020). This has meant returning this control not only from Brussels but also from the devolved administrations in Scotland, Wales and Northern Ireland. There were some initial expectations that devolution would be respected through the Brexit process, even though the mechanisms for doing so were not explicitly stated. However, it appears that after a closer examination of what obligations remained once the UK has withdrawn from the EU treaties, then more fundamental recentralisation could occur under the guise of efficiency and effectiveness associated with the Brexit process. The devolved powers could be gathered to the centre in Whitehall and remove devolutionary practices that have been increasingly introduced over a 20-year period. Will this recentralisation of powers have any longer lasting effects? Chakrabortty (2019) argues that taking this approach could mean the end of the UK, not least because the Brexit process has destroyed the culture of nation building.

Brexit has removed the three basic principles enshrined in EU treaties that have supported the application, implementation and intensification of devolution – fairness, subsidiarity and cohesion – and has been used to remove devolved powers rather than to strengthen them. It appears that recentralisation of the UK state is an intentional outcome of Brexit, but this may be its shortest-lived consequence. The UK COVID-19 pandemic has demonstrated how devolution is working, how people in the devolved nations trust their own leaders more than the PM (Curtice 2020), and how he has been characterised across the UK as the PM of England for the first time. What will be the impact of COVID-19 on devolution? It seems that the pandemic will be more hindrance than help in centralising the UK state but will it hasten the breakup of the Union?

References

Adebowale, V., Alderson, D., Burn, W., Dickson, J., Godlee, F., Goddard, A., et al (2020) Covid-19: call for a rapid forward looking review of the UK's preparedness for a second wave: an open letter to the leaders of all UK political parties, *BMJ*, 369: m2514.

ADPH (2020) Public health leadership, multi-agency capability: guiding principles for effective management of COVID-19 at a local level, 12 June, https://www.adph.org.uk/wp-content/uploads/2020/06/Guiding-Principles-for-Making-Outbreak-Management-Work-Final.pdf, accessed 23 November 2020.

Ahrend, R., Farchy, E., Kaplanis, I. and Lembcke, A. (2014) *What Makes Cities More Productive? Evidence on the Role of Urban Governance from Five OECD Countries*, Paris: OECD.

Alderwick, H. (2020) NHS reorganisation after the pandemic, *BMJ*, 371: m4468, https://www.bmj.com/content/371/bmj.m4468, accessed 22 November 2020.

Anderson, S. (2020) The Johnson government's constitutional reform agenda: prospects and challenges, UCL: the Constitution Unit, 28 February, https://constitution-unit.com/2020/02/28/the-johnson-governments-constitutional-reform-agenda-prospects-and-challenges/, accessed 12 February 2021.

Anthony, G. (2018) Devolution, Brexit, and the Sewel Convention, *Constitution Society*, https://www.consoc.org.uk/wp-content/uploads/2018/04/Gordon-Anthony-Devolution-Brexit-and-the-Sewel-Convention-1.pdf, accessed 17 January 2021.

Arnott, M. (2020) Missing Links: past present and future inter-parliamentary relations in the devolved UK, Institute of Welsh Affairs, https://www.iwa.wales/wp-content/media/Missing-Links-Past-present-and-future-inter-parliamentary-relations-in-the-devolved-UK.pdf, accessed 30 November 2020.

Aroney, N. (2014) Reserved matters, legislative purpose and the referendum on Scottish independence, The University of Queensland, TC Beirne School of Law Legal Studies Research Paper Series, no 13-04, https://papers.ssrn.com/sol3/papers.cfm?abstract_id=2244891#, accessed 28 January 2021.

Ashford, J. (2020) What is a 'federal Britain'? *The Week*, 27 January, https://www.theweek.co.uk/105397/what-is-a-federal-britain, accessed 26 November 2020.

Aven, T. (2015) Implications of black swans to the foundations and practice of risk assessment and management, *Reliability Engineering & System Safety*, 134: 83–91.

Ayres, S., Flinders, M. and Sandford, M. (2018) Territory, power and statecraft: understanding English devolution, *Regional Studies*, 52(6): 853–64.

Baldini, G., Bressanelli, E. and Massetti, E. (2018) Who is in control? Brexit and the Westminster model, *Political Quarterly*, 89(4): 537–44.

Bannink, D. and Ossewaarde, R. (2012) Decentralization: new modes of governance and administrative responsibility, *Administration & Society,* 44(5): 595–624.

Barca, F. (2009) *A Place-based Approach to Meeting European Union Challenges,* Brussels: CEC.

Batchelor, T. (2020) Spotlight on Matt Hancock over appointment of close friend and lobbyist to health role, *The Independent*, 24 November, https://www.independent.co.uk/news/uk/politics/matt-hancock-gina-coladangelo-health-advisor-b1760004.html, accessed 27 November 2020.

BBC (2020a) Coronavirus: libraries see surge in e-book borrowing during lockdown, 22 April, https://www.bbc.co.uk/news/uk-england-52368191, accessed 23 November 2020.

BBC (2020b) Coronavirus: 'mix-up' over EU ventilator scheme, 26 March, https://www.bbc.co.uk/news/uk-politics-52052694, accessed 30 November 2020.

Beaubien, J. (2020) How South Korea reined in the outbreak without shutting everything down, NPR, 26 March, https://www.npr.org/sections/goatsandsoda/2020/03/26/821688981/how-south-korea-reigned-in-the-outbreak-without-shutting-everything-down?t=1605865069104, accessed 20 November 2020.

Bekkers, V., Dijkstra, G. and Fenger, M. (2016) *Governance and the Democratic Deficit: Assessing the Democratic Legitimacy of Governance Practices*, London: Routledge.

Berg, S. (2020) Do-not-resuscitate order: care home use reviewed, BBC News, 12 October, https://www.bbc.co.uk/news/health-54505786, accessed 19 November 2020.

Bhattacharjee, A., Nguyen, D. and Venables, T. (2020) The prospects for regional disparities in the UK in times of Brexit and Covid-19, *National Institute Economic Review*, 253: R1–R3, https://doi.org/10.1017/nie.2020.25.

Blunkett, D. and Flinders, M. (2020) The privilege of public service and the dangers of populist technocracy: a response to Michael Gove and Dominic Cumming's 2020 Ditchley Annual Lecture, *British Politics*, 1–15.

Blunkett, D., Flinders, M. and Prosser, B. (2016) Devolution, evolution, revolution … democracy? What's really happening to English local governance?, *Political Quarterly*, 87(4): 553–64.

Booth, R. (2020) Inquiry begins into blanket use in England of 'do not resuscitate orders', *The Guardian*, 12 October, https://www.theguardian.com/world/2020/oct/12/inquiry-begins-into-blanket-use-in-england-of-covid-do-not-resuscitate-orders, accessed 19 November 2020.

Borghetto, E. and Franchino, F. (2010) The role of subnational authorities in the implementation of EU directives, *Journal of European Public Policy*, 17(6): 759–80.

Bowers, P. (2005) The Sewel Convention, Parliament and Constitutional Centre, Standard Note: SN/PC/2084, 25.

Brazier, R. (2001) How near is a written Constitution, *Northern Ireland Legal Quarterly*, 52(1): 1–19.

Briggs, C.L. (2005) Communicability, racial discourse, and disease, *Annual Review of Anthropology*, 34: 269–91.

Briggs, A., Jenkins, D. and Fraser, F. (2020) NHS Test and Trace: the journey so far. The Health Foundation, 23 September, https://www.health.org.uk/sites/default/files/2020-09/NHS%20Test%20and%20Trace.pdf, accessed 20 November 2020.

Brooks, L., Elgot, J. and Murphy, S. (2020) Devolution 'a disaster north of the border', says Boris Johnson, *The Guardian*, 16 November, https://www.theguardian.com/uk-news/2020/nov/16/scotland-devolution-a-disaster-north-of-the-border-says-boris-johnson, accessed 17 November 2020.

Brown, G. (2020) How to save the United Kingdom, *New Statesman*, 18 November, https://www.newstatesman.com/politics/uk/2020/11/how-save-united-kingdom, accessed 19 January 2020.

Cabinet Office (2012) *Devolution: Memorandum of Understanding and Supplementary Agreement*, London: HMSO.

Cabinet Office (2017) *National Risk Register of Civil Emergencies*, London: Cabinet Office.

Cairney, P. (2006) Venue shift following devolution: when reserved meets devolved in Scotland, *Regional & Federal Studies*, 16(4): 429–45.

Calkin, S. (2020) Jenrick reveals £1.25bn council Covid response spending, *Local Government Chronicle*, 22 May, https://www.lgcplus.com/finance/jenrick-reveals-1-25bn-council-covid-response-spending-22-05-2020/, accessed 22 November 2020.

Calvillo, D.P., Ross, B.J., Garcia, R.J., Smelter, T.J. and Rutchick, A.M. (2020) Political ideology predicts perceptions of the threat of Covid-19 (and susceptibility to fake news about it), *Social Psychological and Personality Science*, https://doi.org/10.1177/1948550620940539.

Camões, P. (2020) Types of decentralisation and governance: evidence from across the world, *Public Affairs*, https://doi.org/10.1002/pa.2435.

Carmichael, P. and Knox, C. (1999) Towards 'a new era'? Some developments in governance of Northern Ireland, *International Review of Administrative Sciences*, 65(1): 103–16.

CEC (2001) European Governance: A White Paper, Brussels: CEC.

CEC (2007) White Paper Together for Health: A Strategic Approach for the EU 2008–2013, Brussels, 23.10.2007 COM(2007) 630 final.

Chakelian, A. (2020) Revealed: the £208m food box rip-off, *New Statesman*, 16 October, https://www.newstatesman.com/politics/uk/2020/10/208m-food-box-rip-off-private-outsource-government-contract-covid-corona-virus, accessed 20 October 2020.

Chakrabortty, A. (2019) Saving the Union will need imagination – and we've lost it, *The Guardian,* 17 October, https://www.theguardian.com/commentisfree/2019/oct/17/salvaging-union-imagination-break-up-uk, accessed 28 January 2021.

Chamberlain, W. (2020) The creation of a federal United Kingdom, *Liberal Democrats,* 26 September, https://www.libdems.org.uk/a20-federal-uk, accessed 26 November 2020.

Chandler, J.A. (2013) *Explaining Local Government: Local Government in Britain since 1800*, Manchester: Manchester University Press.

Charbit C. (2020) From 'de jure' to 'de facto' decentralised public policies: the multi-level governance approach, *British Journal of Politics and International Relations*, https://doi.org/10.1177/1369148120937624.

Cheung A., Paun A. and Valsamidis L. (2019) *Devolution at 20*, London: IfG.

Christensen, T. and Lægreid, P. (2020) Balancing governance capacity and legitimacy: how the Norwegian Government handled the COVID-19 crisis as a high performer, *Public Administration Review*, 80(5): 774–9.

Clarke, S. (2020) Northern Powerhouse Education, Skills, and Employment Summit, 2020 Speech given by the Minister for Regional Growth and Local Government at the Northern Powerhouse Education, Skills, and Employment Summit, 15 July, https://www.public-sector.co.uk/article/a5393966744b47731fe aa4f9f4a51f55, accessed 22 November 2020.

Clifford, B. and Morphet, J. (2015) The British-Irish Council: political expedient or institution in waiting, *Journal of Cross Border Studies in Ireland*, 10: 91–106.

Coakley, J. (2014) British Irish institutional structures: towards a new relationship, *Irish Political Studies*, 29(1): 76–97.

Cole, A. (2006) Decentralization in France: central steering, capacity building and identity construction, *French Politics*, 4(1): 31–57.

Coles, E. (1998) Risk and crisis management in the public sector: what price emergency planning? Local authority civil protection in the UK, *Public Money and Management*, 18(4): 27–32.

Conn, D. (2020) Nurses barred from NHS 111 Covid clinical division after 60% of calls unsafe, *The Guardian*, 1 October, https://www.theguardian.com/world/2020/oct/01/nurses-barred-from-nhs-111-covid-clinical-service-after-60-of-calls-unsafe, accessed 20 November 2020.

Conn, D. and Lawrence F. (2020) NHS deal with Hancock's former neighbour a disgrace, says Labour, *The Guardian*, 26 November, https://www.theguardian.com/world/2020/nov/26/nhs-deal-with-hancocks-former-neighbour-a-disgrace-says-labour, accessed 27 November 2020.

Cookson, R. (2020) Was the scientific advice for lockdown flawed? *BBC News*, 19 November, https://www.bbc.co.uk/news/health-54976192 , accessed 19 November 2020.

Cooper, C. (2020) 'Loathing' of Boris Johnson fuelling surge in support for Scottish independence: poll, *Politico*, 30 October, https://www.politico.eu/article/loathing-of-boris-johnson-fueling-surge-in-support-for-scottish-independence-poll/, accessed 25 November 2020.

Constitution Unit (2020) Working Group on Unification Referendums on the Island of Ireland, Interim Report, London: UCL.

Convery, A. (2013) Devolution and the limits of Tory statecraft: the Conservative Party in coalition and Scotland and Wales, *Parliamentary Affairs*, 67(1): 25–44.

Cosslett, R.L. (2019) Brexit is giving Welsh nationalism a new popular appeal, *The Guardian*, 28 September, https://www.theguardian.com/commentisfree/2019/sep/28/wales-nationalism-brexit-welsh-language, accessed 28 January 2021.

Craigie, R.J., Farrelly, P.J., Santos, R., Smith, S.R., Pollard, J.S. and Jones, D.J. (2020) Manchester Arena bombing: lessons learnt from a mass casualty incident, *BMJ Military Health*, 166(2): 72–5.

Crayne, M.P. and Medeiros, K.E. (2020) Making sense of crisis: charismatic, ideological, and pragmatic leadership in response to COVID-19, *American Psychologist*, http://dx.doi.org/10.1037/amp0000715.

Curtice, J. (2020) Covid in Scotland: how do Scots rate their leaders in the pandemic?, *BBC News*, 19 November, https://www.bbc.co.uk/news/uk-scotland-54973255, accessed 25 November 2020.

Cushion, S., Kyriakidou, M., Morani, M. and Soo, N. (2020) Coronavirus: fake news less of a problem than confusing government messages – new study, *The Conversation*, 12 June, https://theconversation.com/coronavirus-fake-news-less-of-a-problem-than-confusing-government-messages-new-study-140383, accessed 26 November 2020.

Cuthbertson, A. (2020) Coronavirus tracked: how trust in Boris Johnson compares to Trump and other leaders during pandemic, *The Independent*, 21 August, https://www.independent.co.uk/news/uk/home-news/coronavirus-boris-johnson-trump-trust-poll-scott-morrison-a9681956.html, accessed 30 November 2020.

Dahlström, C., Peters, B.G. and Pierre, J. (2011) Steering from the centre: strengthening political control in western democracies, in C. Dahlström, B.G. Peters and J. Pierre (eds) *Steering from the Centre: Strengthening Political Control in Western Democracies*, Toronto: University of Toronto Press, pp 3–26.

Daly, M. (2020) COVID-19 and care homes in England: what happened and why?, *Social Policy & Administration*, 54(7), https://doi.org/10.1111/spol.12645.

Davidson, S. (2017) Public affairs practice and lobbying inequality: reform and regulation of the influence game, *Public Affairs*, 17(4), https://doi.org/10.1002/pa.1665.

Davies, E. and Mackie, P. (2019) Scottish Public Health Network (ScotPHN) The Community Empowerment (Scotland) Act 2015 Parts 3 and 5: What is Public Health's role?, https://www.scotphn. net/wp-content/uploads/2017/10/2019_08_13-CEA-Report-Final.pdf, accessed 23 November 2020.

Davies, R. (2020) Government 'ignores' UK textiles firms desperate to make PPE, *The Guardian*, 16 April, https://www.theguardian. com/fashion/2020/apr/16/government-ignores-uk-textiles-firms-desperate-to-make-ppe, accessed 20 April 2020.

Denham, J. (2020a) Greater Manchester tier 3 rules: what the stand-off tells us about England's centralisation, *British Politics and Policy at LSE*, http://eprints.lse.ac.uk/107343/1/politicsandpolicy_greater_manchester_tier_3_rules_what_the_stand_off.pdf, accessed 25 November 2020.

Denham, J. (2020b) The coronavirus crisis is a moment for England to craft a new national story, *New Statesman*, 23 April, https://www.newstatesman.com/politics/uk/2020/04/coronavirus-crisis-england-national-story-memory, accessed 26 November 2020.

Dijkstra, L. and Poelman, H. (2012) Cities in Europe: the new OECD-EC definition, *Regional Focus*, 1: 1–13.

DoH (2010) *Healthy Lives, Healthy People: Our Strategy for Public Health in England*, vol 7985, London: The Stationery Office.

Doherty, B., Paterson, M., Plows, A. and Wall, D. (2003) Explaining the fuel protests, *British Journal of Politics and International Relations*, 5(1): 1–23.

Donoghue, D. (2020) Unpublished devolution review recommends major Whitehall shakeup, *The Press and Journal*, 30 June, https://www.pressandjournal.co.uk/fp/news/politics/uk-politics/2299679/exclusive-unpublished-devolution-review-recommends-major-whitehall-shakeup/, accessed 17 November 2020.

Dougan, M., Hayward, K., Hunt, J., McEwen, N., McHarg A. and Wincott, D. (2020) *UK Internal Market Bill, Devolution and the Union: UK in a Changing Europe*, London: Kings College London, https://ukandeu.ac.uk/wp-content/uploads/2020/10/UK-internal-Market-Bill-devolution-and-the-union.pdf, accessed 17 November 2020.

Drakeford, M. (2020) Boris Johnson's inaction has forced me to ban travel to Wales from England's Covid hotspots, *The Guardian*, 15 October, https://www.theguardian.com/commentisfree/2020/oct/15/boris-johnson-wales-england-covid-hotspots-prime-minister, accessed 18 January 2020.

Dunton, J. (2020) Watchdog sounds alarm over rising political bias in public appointments, *Civil Service World*, 5 November, https://www.civilserviceworld.com/news/article/watchdog-sounds-alarm-over-rising-political-bias-in-public-appointments, accessed 20 November 2020.

Egeberg, M. and Trondal, J. (2009) Political leadership and bureaucratic autonomy: effects of agencification, *Governance*, 22(4): 673–88.

Evans, Lord (2020) The Hugh Kay Lecture: Are we in a post-Nolan age?, 12 November, https://www.gov.uk/government/speeches/the-hugh-kay-lecture-are-we-in-a-post-nolan-age, accessed 20 November 2020.

Farrell, C., Law, J. and Thomas, S. (2020) Public health and local government in Wales: every policy a health policy – a collaborative agenda, in A. Bonner (ed), *Local Authorities and the Social Determinants of Health*, Bristol: Policy Press, pp 385–400.

Ferry, M., Kah, S. and Bachtler, J. (2018) Integrated territorial development: new instruments – new results, IQ-net thematic paper, 42(2), https://strathprints.strath.ac.uk/69564/, accessed 11 February 2021.

Fleischer, J. (2011) Steering for the German centre: more policy coordination fewer policy initiatives, in C. Dahlström, B.G. Peters and J. Pierre (eds), *Steering from the Centre: Strengthening Political Control in Western Democracies*, Toronto: University of Toronto Press, pp 54–79.

Fraser C. and Briggs, A. (2020) NHS Test and Trace performance tracker, The Health Foundation, 19 November, https://www. health.org.uk/news-and-comment/charts-and-infographics/nhs-test-and-trace-performance-tracker, accessed 25 November 2020.

Freedman, L. (2020) Scientific advice at a time of emergency: SAGE and Covid-19, *Political Quarterly*, 91(3): 514–22.

Gallagher, S. (2019) Speech to Planning Officers, Annual Conference, Nottingham, 4 July.

Gamble A. (2015) Austerity as statecraft, *Parliamentary Affairs*, 68(1): 42–57.

Garikipati, S. and Kambhampati, U. (2020) Leading the fight against the pandemic: does gender 'really' matter?, *SSRN*, http://dx.doi. org/10.2139/ssrn.3617953, accessed 25 November 2020.

Gilbert, D. and Clark, A. (2020) Scottish Independence tracker: polls put support at highest level since 2014 vote, *The Telegraph,* 13 November, https://www.telegraph.co.uk/news/0/scottish-independence-tracker-polls-show-support-time-high/, accessed 17 November 2020.

Glasson, J. and Marshall, T. (2007) *Regional Planning*, London: Routledge.

Goetz, K.H. and Meyer-Sahling, J.H. (2009) Political time in the EU: dimensions, perspectives, theories, *Journal of European Public Policy*, 16(2): 180–201.

Gove, M. (2020) The privilege of public service, Ditchley Annual Lecture, 27 June, https://www.gov.uk/government/speeches/ the-privilege-of-public-service-given-as-the-ditchley-annual-lecture, accessed 28 January 2021.

Grant, M. (1993) The return of local government: the Banham Commission, in A. Duff (ed), *Subsidiarity within the European Union,* London: Federal Trust for Education and Research, pp 107–9.

Greenhalgh, T. (2020) Face coverings for the public: laying straw men to rest, *Journal of Evaluation in Clinical Practice*, 26(4), https:// doi.org/10.1111/jep.13415.

Greer, S.L. (2005) The territorial bases of health policymaking in the UK after devolution, *Regional & Federal Studies*, 15(4): 501–18.

Gregory, A. (2005) Communication dimensions of the UK foot and mouth disease crisis, 2001, *Public Affairs*, 5(3–4): 312–28.

Halliday, J. and Pidd, H. (2020) English councils with highest Covid rates launch own test-and-trace systems, *The Guardian*, 4 August, https://www.theguardian.com/society/2020/aug/04/english-councils-with-highest-covid-rates-launch-own-test-and-trace-systems, accessed 23 November 2020.

Ham, C. (2020) Testing and contact tracing: a role for local leaders, *Health Services Journal*, 5 May, https://www.hsj.co.uk/technology-and-innovation/testing-and-contact-tracing-a-role-for-local-leaders/7027567.article, accessed 20 November 2020.

Hamlin, C. (1998) *Public Health and Social Justice in the Age of Chadwick: Britain, 1800–1854*, Cambridge: Cambridge University Press.

Harris, L. and Rutter, J. (2015) *Centre Forward: Effective Support for the Prime Minister at the Centre of Government*, London: IfG.

Hayward, W. (2020) Covid, Brexit and Welsh independence: do you want an independent Wales?, *Walesonline*, 30 October, https://www.walesonline.co.uk/news/wales-news/covid-brexit-welsh-independence-would-19187484, accessed 25 November 2020.

Hazell, R. (2005) Devolution as a legislative partnership, in R. Hazell and R. Rawlings (eds), *Law Making and the Constitution*, Exeter: Imprint Academic, pp 295–318.

Hazell, R. (2006) The English Question, *Publius: The Journal of Federalism*, 36(1): 37–56.

Heald, D. and McLeod, A. (2002) Beyond Barnett? Funding devolution, in J. Adams and P. Robinson (eds), *Devolution in Practice: Public Policy Differences Within the UK*, London: Institute for Public Policy Research, pp 147–75.

Heenan, D. (2009) Working across borders to promote positive mental health and well-being, *Disability & Society,* 24(6): 715–26.

Heenan, D. (2020) Healthy co-dependencies: co-ordination across borders in response to COVID-19 and beyond Brexit, *Journal of Cross Border Studies in Ireland*, 15: 73–87.

Hendry, A., Haigh, I., Nicholls, R., Winter, H., Neal, R., Wahl, T., Joly-Laugel, A. and Darby, S. (2019) Assessing the characteristics and drivers of compound flooding events around the UK coast, *Hydrology and Earth System Sciences*, 23: 3117–39.

Henley, J. (2020) Female-led countries handled coronavirus better, study suggests, *The Guardian*, 18 August, https://www. theguardian.com/world/2020/aug/18/female-led-countries-handled-coronavirus-better-study-jacinda-ardern-angela-merkel, accessed 25 November 2020.

Héritier, A. and Lehmkuhl, D. (2008) Introduction: the shadow of hierarchy and new modes of governance, *Journal of Public Policy*, 28(1): 1–17.

Hern, A. (2020) 'Eat out to help out' may have caused sixth of Covid clusters over summer, *The Guardian*, 30 October, https:// www.theguardian.com/business/2020/oct/30/treasury-rejects-theory-eat-out-to-help-out-caused-rise-in-covid, accessed 27 November 2020.

HMG (1968) Committee on the Civil Service, *The Civil Service: Report of the Committee, 1966-68*, The Fulton Report HM Stationery Office.

HMG (2019a) *The Dunlop Review into UK Government Union Capability*, London: HMG.

HMG (2019b) Queen's Speech December 2019: background briefing notes, 19 December, https://www.gov.uk/government/publications/queens-speech-december-2019-background-briefing-notes, accessed 22 November 2020.

Home Office (2018) *Biological Security Strategy*, London: Home Office.

Honeycombe-Foster, M. (2020) Ministers promise 'power surge' to devolved nations after Brexit amid bitter row with Scotland and Wales, *Politicshome*, 16 July, https://www.politicshome. com/news/article/ministers-promise-power-surge-to-devolved-nations-after-brexit-amid-bitter-row-with-scotland-and-wales, accessed 17 November 2020.

Hooghe, L., Marks, G. and Marks, G.W. (2001) *Multi-level Governance and European Integration*, Washington, DC: Rowman & Littlefield.

Huang, S.K., Lindell, M.K., Prater, C.S., Wu, H.C. and Siebeneck, L.K. (2012) Household evacuation decision making in response to Hurricane Ike, *Natural Hazards Review*, 13(4): 283–96.

Iacobucci, G. (2020) Covid-19: lack of PPE in care homes is risking spread of virus, leaders warn, *BMJ*, 368: m1280, https://www.bmj.com/content/368/bmj.m1280.long, accessed 23 November 2020.

Illman, J. (2020) NHS block books almost all private hospital sector capacity to fight covid-19, *Health Service Journal*, 21 March, https://www.hsj.co.uk/policy-and-regulation/nhs-block-books-almost-all-private-hospital-sector-capacity-to-fight-covid-19/7027196.article, accessed 20 November 2020.

IPS (2020) Strategies for managing acute shortages of personal protective equipment during the COVID-19 pandemic, 23 April, file:///C:/Users/Janice/Downloads/Strategies_for_PPE_shortages_23_4_20_Final.pdf, accessed 20 November 2020.

IpsosMORI (2020) Half of Britons think second lockdown in England will be effective in reducing spread of COVID-19, https://www.ipsos.com/ipsos-mori/en-uk/half-britons-think-second-lockdown-england-will-be-effective-reducing-spread-covid-19, accessed 30 November 2020.

Jamet, J.F. (2011) The optimal assignment of prerogatives to different levels of government in the EU, *Journal of Common Market Studies*, 49(3): 563–84.

Jeffrey, C. (2007) The unfinished business of devolution: seven open questions, *Public Policy and Administration*, 22: 92–108.

Jenkin, B. (2020) Inter-parliamentary relations: missing links? Podcast, 22 September, Institute of Welsh Affairs, https://www.iwa.wales/eventbrite-event/inter-parliamentary-relations-missing-links/, accessed 30 November 2020.

Johnson, B. (2020) Keynote speech to Conservative Party Conference, 6 October, https://www.conservatives.com/news/boris-johnson-read-the-prime-ministers-keynote-speech-in-full, accessed 20 November 2020.

Jones, P., Wynn, M., Hillier, D. and Comfort, D. (2017) A commentary on the city deals in the UK, *Public Affairs*, 17(3): e1661, https://onlinelibrary.wiley.com/doi/abs/10.1002/pa.1661, accessed 17 November 2020.

Judge, A. and Maltby, T. (2017) European Energy Union? Caught between securitisation and 'riskification', *European Journal of International Security*, 2(2): 179–202.

Kauppi, N. (2018) *Democracy, Social Resources and Political Power in the European Union*, Manchester: Manchester University Press.

Keating, M. (2019) *The Repatriation of Competences in Agriculture after Brexit*, Edinburgh: Centre for Constitutional Change.

Kenny, M. and Sheldon, J. (2020) When planets collide: the British Conservative Party and the discordant goals of delivering Brexit and preserving the domestic Union, 2016–2019, *Political Studies*, https://doi.org/10.1177/0032321720930986.

Kerslake, R. (2020) UK 2070 Commission Final Report, Make No Little Plans, http://uk2070.org.uk/wp-content/uploads/2020/02/UK2070-EXEC-SUMMARY-FINAL-REPORT.pdf, accessed 27 November 2020.

Kingdon, J.W. (2013) *Agendas, Alternatives, and Public Policies*, vol 45, 2nd edn, Boston: Little, Brown, pp 165–9.

Kirrage, D., Reynolds, G., Smith, G.E. and Olowokure, B. (2007) Investigation of an outbreak of Legionnaires' disease: Hereford, UK 2003, *Respiratory Medicine*, 101(8): 1639–44.

Krugman, P.R. (1991) *Geography and Trade*, Cambridge, MA: MIT Press.

Labour Policy Forum (2019) Local Economic Development, https://www.policyforum.labour.org.uk/commissions/local-economic-development, accessed 17 January 2021.

Ladhani, S.N., Chow, J.Y., Janarthanan, R., Fok, J., Crawley-Boevey, E., Vusirikala, A., et al (2020) Increased risk of SARS-CoV-2 infection in staff working across different care homes: enhanced CoVID-19 outbreak investigations in London care homes, *Journal of Infection*, 81(4): 621–4.

Laffin, M. and Shaw, E. (2007) British devolution and the Labour Party: how a national party adapts to devolution, *British Journal of Politics and International Relations*, 9(1): 55–72.

Law, S. (2020) Thousands sign Nicola Sturgeon briefing petition to stop BBC binning broadcast, *Daily Record*, 11 September, https://www.dailyrecord.co.uk/news/scottish-news/nicola-sturgeon-coronavirus-briefing-bbc-22665326, accessed 25 November 2020.

Leigh, M. (2019) Anticipating and preventing emergencies, Emergency Planning College, Occasional Paper 22.

Leyland, P. (2011) The multifaceted constitutional dynamics of UK devolution, *International Journal of Constitutional Law*, 9(1): 251–73.

LGA (2020a) *COVID-19 Outbreak Councillor Guidance, 24 March*, London: LGA.

LGA (2020b) *COVID-19 Outbreak: Reset and Recovery Councillor Guidance, July*, London: LGA.

LGA (2020c) *Re-thinking Local, June*, London: LGA.

LGA (2020d) Remote council meetings: case studies: case studies hub, https://www.local.gov.uk/our-support/guidance-and-resources/remote-council-meetings/case-studies, accessed 28 January 2021.

LGA (2020e) COVID-19: good council practice: case study hub, https://www.local.gov.uk/covid-19-good-council-practice, accessed 28 January 2021.

LGA (2020f) *Changes to the Planning System as a Result of the COVID19 Pandemic June 2020*, https://www.local.gov.uk/sites/default/files/documents/LGA%20briefing%20-%20Changes%20to%20the%20planning%20system%20in%20response%20to%20the%20COVID-19%20pandemic.pdf, accessed 23 November 2020.

Lorne, C., McDonald, R., Walshe, K., and Coleman, A. (2019) Regional assemblage and the spatial reorganisation of health and care: the case of devolution in Greater Manchester, England, *Sociology of Health & Illness*, 41(7): 1236–50.

Loughlin, J. (1996) Representing regions in Europe: the Committee of the Regions, *Regional & Federal Studies*, 6(2): 147–65.

Lowndes, V. and Gardner, A. (2016) Local governance under the Conservatives: super-austerity, devolution and the 'smarter state', *Local Government Studies*, 42(3): 357–75.

Lynch, P. and Hopkins, S. (2001) The British-Irish Council: progress frustrated, *Regional Studies*, 35(8): 753–8.

Machin, D. and Mayr, A. (2013) Corporate crime and the discursive deletion of responsibility: a case study of the Paddington rail crash, *Crime, Media, Culture*, 9(1): 63-82.

MacKinnon, D. (2015) Devolution, state restructuring and policy divergence in the UK, *Geographical Journal*, 181(1): 47–56.

MacLeod, G. (2018) The Grenfell Tower atrocity: exposing urban worlds of inequality, injustice, and an impaired democracy, *City*, 22(4): 460–89.

MacMath, J. (2020) First Minister Mark Drakeford is living in a 'miniature hut' at the bottom of his garden, *walesonline*, 30 July, https://www.walesonline.co.uk/news/wales-news/first-minister-mark-drakeford-living-18689082, accessed 25 November 2020.

Maddox, B. (2020) Reform of the centre of government, *IfG Insight July*, London: IfG.

Manderson, L. and Levine, S. (2020) COVID-19: risk, fear and fallout, *Medical Anthropology*, 39(5): 367–70.

Marks, L., Hunter, D.J., Scalabrini, S., Gray, J., McCafferty, S., Payne, N., Peckham, S., Salway, S. and Thokala, P. (2015) The return of public health to local government in England: changing the parameters of the public health prioritization debate?, *Public Health*, 129(9): 1194–203.

Marlow, D. (2019) Local Enterprise Partnerships: seven-year itch, or in need of a radical re-think? Lessons from Cambridgeshire and Peterborough, UK, *Local Economy*, 34(2): 139–48.

Marsh, D. (1994) *Joseph Chamberlain: Entrepreneur in Politics*, New Haven, CT, and London: Yale University Press.

Marsh, D. (2010) Stability and change: the last dualism?, *Critical Policy Studies*, 4(1): 86–101.

May, T. (2019) PM speech on the Union, 4 July, https://www.gov.uk/government/speeches/pm-speech-on-the-union-4-july-2019, accessed 28 November 2020.

Mason, K.A. (2012) Mobile migrants, mobile germs: migration, contagion and boundary building in Shenzhen, China after SARS, *Medical Anthropology*, 31(2): 112–31.

McAllister, L. (2000) Devolution and the new context for public policy-making: lessons from the EU structural funds in Wales, *Public Policy and Administration*, 15(2): 38–52.

McConnell, A. (2003) Overview: crisis management, influences, responses and evaluation, *Parliamentary Affairs*, 56(3): 363–409.

McCrudden, C. (2015) State architecture: subsidiarity, devolution, federalism and independence, in M. Elliott and D. Feldman (eds), *The Cambridge Companion to Public Law*, Cambridge: Cambridge University Press, pp 193–214.

McEwen, N. and Redmond, A. (2019) *The Repatriation of Competences in Climate and Energy Policy after Brexit*, Edinburgh: Centre for Constitutional Change.

McEwen, N., Kenny, M., Sheldon, J. and Swan, C. (2020) Intergovernmental relations in the UK: time for a radical overhaul?, *Political Quarterly*, 91(3): 632–40.

McGrattan, C. and Williams, S. (2017) Devolution and identity: multidirectionality in 'Welshness' and 'Northern Irishness', *Regional & Federal Studies*, 27(4): 465–82.

McGregor-Lowndes, M. and Ryan, C. (2009) Reducing the compliance burden of non-profit organisations: cutting red tape, *Australian Journal of Public Administration*, 68(1): 21–38.

McGuire, D., Cunningham, J.E., Reynolds, K. and Matthews-Smith, G. (2020) Beating the virus: an examination of the crisis communication approach taken by New Zealand Prime Minister Jacinda Ardern during the Covid-19 pandemic, *Human Resource Development International*, 23(4): 361–79.

McHarg, A. (2018) Navigating without maps: constitutional silence and the management of the Brexit crisis, *International Journal of Constitutional Law*, 16(3): 952–68.

McHarg, A. and Mitchell, J. (2017) Brexit and Scotland, *British Journal of Politics and International Relations*, 19(3): 512–26.

McLeish, C. and Nightingale, P. (2007) Biosecurity, bioterrorism and the governance of science: the increasing convergence of science and security policy, *Research Policy*, 36(10): 1635–54.

MacPhail, E. (2009) PSA Annual Conference, Manchester 2009: Exploiting the European Union as a political opportunity structure? Understanding the Scottish Executive's engagement with the EU 1999–2007.

Melding, D. (2007) *Will Britain Survive Beyond 2020?* Cardiff: Institute for Welsh Affairs.

MHCLG (2017) *Review of Local Enterprise Partnership Governance and Transparency*, London: MHCLG.

MHCLG (2020) *Planning for the Future*, London: MHCLG.

Millar, D. and Scott, A. (1993) Subsidiarity and Scotland, in A. Duff (ed), *Subsidiarity within the European Community*, London: The Federal Trust, pp 87–104.

Mitchell, J. (2004) Understanding Stormont-London Relations, ESRC Devolution and Constitutional Change Research Programme, https://www.researchgate.net/profile/James_Mitchell13/publication/242322693_Understanding_Stormont-London_Relations/links/53fe1db70cf23bb019be00d0/Understanding-Stormont-London-Relations.pdf, accessed 17 January 2021.

Morphet, J. (1994) The committee of the regions, *Local Government Policy Making*, 20: 56–56.

Morphet, J. (2007) *Modern Local Government*, London: Sage.

Morphet J. (2013) *How Europe Shapes British Public Policy*, Bristol: Policy Press.

Morphet, J. (2017) *Beyond Brexit*, Bristol: Policy Press.

Morphet, J. (2021a) *Outsourcing in the UK: Policies, Practices and Outcomes,* Bristol: Policy Press.

Morphet, J. (2021b) Public value management in Brexit Britain, in J. Connolly and A. van der Zwet (eds), *Public Value Management, Governance and Reform in Britain,* Cham: Palgrave Macmillan, pp 227–57.

Morphet, J. and Clifford, B. (2018) 'Who else would we speak to?' National Policy Networks in post-devolution Britain: the case of spatial planning, *Public Policy and Administration*, 33(1): 3–21.

Morphet, J. and Clifford, B. (2020) *Reviving Local Authority Housing Delivery: Challenging Austerity Through Municipal Entrepreneurialism*, Bristol: Policy Press.

Mount, F. (2020a) Après Brexit, *London Review of Books,* 20 February, 42(4), https://www.lrb.co.uk/the-paper/v42/n04/ferdinand-mount/apres-brexit, accessed 5 February 2021.

Mount, F. (2020b) Superman falls to earth, *London Review of Books*, 42(13): 3–7.

Moynihan, D.P. (2006) Ambiguity in policy lessons: the agencification experience. *Public Administration*, 84(4): 1029–50.

Mullen, T. (2019) Brexit and the territorial governance of the United Kingdom, *Contemporary Social Science*, 14(2): 276–93.

Murdoch, Z., Connolly, S. and Kassim, H. (2018) Administrative legitimacy and the democratic deficit of the European Union, *Journal of European Public Policy*, 25(3): 389–408.

Murphie, A. (2019) In perspective: setting up new Combined Authorities in England: A National Audit Office assessment, *Local Economy*, 34(2): 94–105.

Murphy, S. (2020a) More than 500,000 people sign up to be NHS volunteers, *The Guardian*, 25 March, https://www.theguardian.com/world/2020/mar/25/astonishing-170000-people-sign-up-to-be-nhs-volunteers-in-15-hours-coronavirus, accessed 19 November 2020.

Murphy, S. (2020b) Alex Allan: the veteran windsurfing mandarin who quit over Patel row, *The Guardian*, 20 November, https://www.theguardian.com/politics/2020/nov/20/alex-allan-the-veteran-windsurfing-mandarin-who-quit-over-bullying, accessed 27 November 2020.

NAO (2013) *Emergency Planning in the NHS*, London: NAO.

NAO (2017) *Progress in Setting Up Combined Authorities*, London: NAO.

NAO (2018) *Financial Sustainability of Local Authorities 2018*, London: NAO.

NAO (2019) *Progress Delivering the Emergency Services Network*, London: NAO.

NAO (2020a) *Investigation into the Bounce Back Loan Scheme*, London: NAO.

NAO (2020b) *Investigation into How Government Increased the Number of Ventilators Available to the NHS in Response to COVID-19*, London: NAO.

NAO (2020c) *Procurement for COVID-19*, London: NAO.

NAO (2020d) *Readying the NHS and Adult Social Care in England for COVID-19*, London: NAO.

NAO (2020e) *The Supply of Personal Protective Equipment (PPE) During the COVID-19 Pandemic*, London: NAO.

Naylor, C. and Wellings, D. (2019) *A Citizen-Led Approach to Health and Care: Lessons from the Wigan Deal*, London: The Kings Fund.

Newton, K. (2020) Government communications, political trust and compliant social behaviour: the politics of Covid-19 in Britain, *Political Quarterly*, 91(3): 502–13.

Ney, M. (2018) *Review of LEPs*, London: MHCLG.

Norton, P. (2017) *Reform of the House of Lords*, Oxford: Oxford University Press.

O'Brien, P. and Pike, A. (2015) City deals, decentralisation and the governance of local infrastructure funding and financing in the UK, *National Institute Economic Review*, 233(1): R14–R26.

OBR (2020) COVID-19 Scenarios, https://obr.uk/coronavirus-analysis/, accessed 17 January 2021.

O'Carroll, L. (2020) Government admits new Brexit bill will break international law, *The Guardian*, 8 September, https://www.theguardian.com/politics/2020/sep/08/government-admits-new-brexit-bill-will-break-international-law, accessed 27 November 2020.

OECD (2001) *Devolution and Globalisation: Implications for Local Decision-makers*, Paris: OECD.

OECD (2013) *Definition of Functional Urban Areas (FUA) for the OECD Metropolitan Database*, Paris: OECD.

OECD (2017) Globalisation of risk, *Trends Shaping Education Spotlights*, OECD: Paris, https://doi.org/10.1787/44a19295-en.

OECD (2020) *Enhancing Productivity in UK Core Cities Policy Highlights Connecting Local and Regional Growth*, Paris: OECD.

Oliver, D. (2003) *Constitutional Reform in the United Kingdom*, Oxford: Oxford University Press.

Osborne, D. and Gaebler, T. (1993) *Reinventing Government: The Five Strategies for Reinventing Government*, New York: Penguin.

Osborne, G. (2014) Speech to Conservative Party Conference, 4 October.

Page A. (2010) *Making and Breaking Whitehall Departments*, London: IfG, https://www.instituteforgovernment.org.uk/sites/default/files/publications/making_and_breaking_whitehall_departments.pdf, accessed 19 November 2020.

Page, E. (1991) *Localism and Centralism in Europe: The Political and Legal Basis of Local Self-Government*, Oxford: Oxford University Press.

Paul, S. (1999) UK emergency planning: the integrated approach, *Australian Journal of Emergency Management*, 13(4): 47–9.

Paun, A., Kidney Bishop, T., Valsamidis, L. and de Costa, A. (2019) *Ministers Reflect on Devolution: Lessons From 20 Years of Scottish and Welsh Government*, London: IfG.

Payne, S. Parker, G., Foster, P. and Pickard, J. (2020) Top UK government lawyer quits over Brexit withdrawal agreement changes, *Financial Times*, 8 September, https://www.ft.com/content/6186bf1c-055b-4de6-a643-4eea763e1b94, accessed 27 November 2020.

Pazos-Vidal, S. (2019) *Subsidiarity and EU Multilevel Governance: Actors, Networks and Agendas*, London: Routledge.

Pegg, D. (2020) Official report that said UK was not prepared for pandemic is published, *The Guardian*, 22 October, https://www.theguardian.com/world/2020/oct/22/official-report-exercise-cygnus-uk-was-not-prepared-for-pandemic-is-published, accessed 19 November 2020.

Pemberton, S. and Morphet, J. (2014) The rescaling of economic governance: insights into the transitional territories of England, *Urban Studies*, 51(11): 2354–70.

PHE (2020) How local tracing partnerships are supporting NHS Test and Trace, 19 October, https://publichealthmatters.blog.gov.uk/2020/10/19/how-local-tracing-partnerships-are-supporting-nhs-test-and-trace/, accessed 23 November 2020.

Pickard, J. (2020) Government threatens to take direct control of Transport for London, *Financial Times*, 20 October, https://www.ft.com/content/fc7ad30a-a23b-49fc-a254-643ea6237ed2, accessed 17 November 2020.

Pike, A., Marlow, D., McCarthy, A., O'Brien, P. and Tomaney, J. (2013) Local institutions and local economic growth: the state of the Local Enterprise Partnerships (LEPs) in England: a national survey, University of Newcastle Spatial Economics Research Centre, e-print, https://eprint.ncl.ac.uk/196448, accessed 28 January 2021.

Pitt, M. (2007) Learning lessons from the 2007 floods, Independent Review, https://webarchive.nationalarchives.gov.uk/20100812084907/http://archive.cabinetoffice.gov.uk/pittreview/_/media/assets/www.cabinetoffice.gov.uk/flooding_review/pitt_review_full%20pdf.pdf, accessed 22 November 2020.

Pittock, M. (1998) *Jacobitism*, Macmillan International Higher Education, London: Red Globe Press.

Pollak, A. (2020) North-South cooperation on healthcare during a time of Coronavirus, *Journal of Cross Border Studies in Ireland*, 15: 63–72.

Pollitt, C., Birchall, J. and Putman, K. (2016) *Decentralising Public Service Management*, Macmillan International Higher Education, London: Red Globe Press.

Pollock, K. (2017) Local interoperability in UK emergency management, Research Report, Emergency Planning College Occasional Paper 19.

Pycroft, C. (1995) Restructuring local government: the Banham Commission's failed historic enterprise, *Public Policy and Administration*, 10(1): 49–62.

Quinn, A. (2020) NI Executive set for second Stormont showdown next week as scientific advice set to clash with economy – Nine additional deaths recorded in last 24 hours – Arlene Foster rules out closing schools early for Christmas, *The Newsletter*, 17 November, https://www.newsletter.co.uk/health/coronavirus/ni-executive-set-second-stormont-showdown-next-week-scientific-advise-set-clash-economy-nine-additional-deaths-recorded-last-24-hours-arlene-foster-rules-out-closing-schools-early-christmas-3038118, accessed 25 November.

Radnor, Z. and Walley, P. (2008) Learning to walk before we try to run: adapting lean for the public sector, *Public Money and Management*, 28(1): 13–20.

Rallings, C. and Thrasher, M. (2006) 'Just another expensive talking shop': public attitudes and the 2004 Regional Assembly Referendum in the North East of England, *Regional Studies*, 40(8): 927–36.

Reichborn-Kjennerud, K. and Vabo, S.I. (2017) Extensive decentralisation: but in the shadow of hierarchy, in J. Ruano and M. Profiloru (eds), *The Palgrave Handbook of Decentralisation in Europe*, Cham: Palgrave Macmillan, pp 253–72.

Remuzzi, A. and Remuzzi, G. (2020) COVID-19 and Italy: what next?, *The Lancet*, 395(10231): 1225–8.

Reuters (2020) Brexit talks: Joe Biden says UK and Ireland must not have hard border, *The Guardian*, 25 November, https://www.theguardian.com/politics/2020/nov/25/brexit-talks-joe-biden-says-uk-ireland-border-must-remain-open, accessed 25 November 2020.

Rhodes, R.A.W. (2018) *Control and Power in Central-Local Government Relations*, London: Routledge.

Richards, D. and Smith, M. (2017) 'Things were better in the past': Brexit and the Westminster fallacy of democratic nostalgia, *British Politics and Policy at LSE*, https://blogs.lse.ac.uk/politicsandpolicy/brexit-and-the-westminster-fallacy-of-democratic-nostalgia/, accessed 17 January 2021.

Richards, D., Diamond, P. and Wager, A. (2019) Westminster's Brexit paradox: the contingency of the 'old' versus 'new' politics, *British Journal of Politics and International Relations*, 21(2): 330–48.

RSA (2021) One Powerhouse spatial plans for England, https://www.thersa.org/reports/one-powerhouse, accessed 5 February 2021.

Russell, M. and Sheldon, J. (2018) Options for an English Parliament, UCL Constitutional Unit, https://www.ucl.ac.uk/constitution-unit/sites/constitution-unit/files/179-options-for-an-english-parliament.pdf, accessed 27 November 2020.

Rutter, J. (2020) The government is under attack for its post-Brexit power hoarding ambitions, IfG, 3 November, https://www.instituteforgovernment.org.uk/blog/government-post-brexit-power, accessed 28 January 2021.

Sandford, M. (2013) The abolition of regional government, House of Commons Standard Note: SN/PC/05842, 27 March.

Sandford, M. (2015) *The Bellwin Scheme*, London: House of Commons Library.

Sandford, M. (2017) Signing up to devolution: the prevalence of contract over governance in English devolution policy, *Regional & Federal Studies*, 27(1): 63–82.

Sandford, M. (2019) Money talks: the finances of English Combined Authorities, *Local Economy*, 34(2): 106–22.

Sandford, M. and Gormley-Heenan, C. (2020) 'Taking back control', the UK's constitutional narrative and Schrodinger's devolution, *Parliamentary Affairs*, 73(1): 108–126.

Sargeant J. (2020) *Co-ordination and Divergence: Devolution and Coronavirus*, IfG Insights, October, London: IfG.

Scally, G., Jacobson, B. and Abbasi, K. (2020) The UK's public health response to Covid-19, *BMJ*, 369: m1932, https://www.bmj.com/content/369/bmj.m1932.full, accessed 22 November 2020.

Scambler, G. (2020) Covid-19 as a 'breaching experiment': exposing the fractured society, *Health Sociology Review*, 29(2): 140–8.

Scottish Government (2020a) Coronavirus (COVID-19): test, trace, isolate, support strategy, 4 May, https://www.gov.scot/publications/coronavirus-covid-19-test-trace-isolate-support/pages/6/, accessed 22 November 2020.

Scottish Government (2020b) Coronavirus (COVID-19): local protection levels, 18 November, https://www.gov.scot/publications/coronavirus-covid-19-protection-levels/, accessed 22 November 2020.

Settle, M. (2020) Rifkind: devolved settlement becoming out-of-date; it's time to consider federal Union, *The Herald*, 22 November, https://www.heraldscotland.com/news/18889524.malcolm-rifkind-devolved-settlement-becoming-out-of-date-time-consider-federal-union/, accessed 26 November 2020.

Sharman, L. (2020) Councils to be fully funded for coronavirus costs, *LocalGov*, 18 March, https://www.localgov.co.uk/-Councils-to-be-fully-funded-for-coronavirus-costs/50205, accessed 22 November 2020.

Schütze, R. (2009) Subsidiarity after Lisbon: reinforcing the safeguards of federalism?, *The Cambridge Law Journal*, 68(3): 525–36.

Seldon, A. and Meakin, J. (2016) *The Cabinet Office, 1916–2018: The Birth of Modern Government*, Hull: Biteback Publishing.

Shao, W. and Hao, F. (2020) Confidence in political leaders can slant risk perceptions of COVID-19 in a highly polarized environment, *Social Science & Medicine*, 261: 113235.

Shao, W., Xian, S., Lin, N., Kunreuther, H., Jackson, N. and Goidel, K. (2017) Understanding the effects of past flood events and perceived and estimated flood risks on individuals' voluntary flood insurance purchase behavior, *Water Research*, 108: 391–400.

Shaw, K. and Robinson, F. (2007) The end of the beginning? Taking forward local democratic renewal in the post-referendum North East, *Local Economy*, 22(3): 243–60.

Smith, B.C. (1985) *Decentralization: The Territorial Dimension of the State*, London: George Allen and Unwin.

Smith, M. (2011) The paradoxes of Britain's strong centre: delegating decisions and reclaiming control, in C. Dahlström, B.G. Peters and J. Pierre (eds), *Steering from the Centre: Strengthening Political Control in Western Democracies*, Toronto: University of Toronto Press, pp 166–90.

Smoke, P. (2015) Rethinking decentralization: assessing challenges to a popular public sector reform, *Public Administration and Development*, 35(2): 97–112.

Solar, C. and Smith, M. (2020) Decentralisation and central-local relations: the case of policing and mental health in England, *British Politics*, 1–18, https://doi.org/10.1057/s41293-019-00132-5.

Stafford, M. (2020) King of the North: Andy Burnham vs Boris Johnson, PSA Blog, https://www.psa.ac.uk/psa/news/king-north-andy-burnham-vs-boris-johnson, accessed 20 October 2020.

Stephens, L. (2020) Wales' test and trace system is working significantly better than England's, *walesonline*, 10 September, https://www.walesonline.co.uk/news/wales-news/wales-test-trace-system-working-18910956, accessed 22 November 2020.

Stoddart, K. (2016) UK cyber security and critical national infrastructure protection, *International Affairs*, 92(5): 1079–105.

Sunak, R. (2020) Spending Review 2020 speech, 25 November, London: HMT.

Syal, R. (2020a) UK's vaccine taskforce chief shared sensitive documents in US, report says, *The Guardian*, 2 November, https://www.theguardian.com/world/2020/nov/02/uks-vaccine-taskforce-chief-shared-sensitive-documents-in-us-report-says, accessed 20 November 2020.

Syal, R. (2020b) Kate Bingham: well-connected but under-fire UK vaccines chief, *The Guardian*, 10 November, https://www.theguardian.com/world/2020/nov/10/kate-bingham-well-connected-but-under-fire-uk-vaccines-chief, accessed 20 November 2020.

Syal, R. (2020c) Chief nurse was dropped from briefings after refusing to back Cummings, *The Guardian*, 20 July, https://www.theguardian.com/politics/2020/jul/20/englands-chief-nurse-dropped-from-covid-19-briefing-after-refusing-to-back-cummings-ruth-may, accessed 25 November 2020.

Syal, R. (2020d) Inquiry raises concerns over how £3.6bn towns fund was distributed, 11 November, https://www.theguardian.com/politics/2020/nov/11/inquiry-raises-concerns-over-how-36bn-towns-fund-was-distributed, accessed 27 November 2020.

Sykes, O. (2018) Post-geography worlds, new dominions, left behind regions, and 'other' places: unpacking some spatial imaginaries of the UK's 'Brexit' debate, *Space and Polity*, 22(2): 137–61.

Tatham, M. (2008) Going solo: direct regional representation in the European Union, *Regional & Federal Studies*, 18(5): 493–515.

Theakston, K. (2016) *Leadership in Whitehall*, London: Palgrave Macmillan.

The Economist (2020) Dominic Cummings and the unchained minsters, *The Economist*, 21 November, https://www.economist.com/britain/2020/11/19/dominic-cummings-and-the-unchained-ministers, accessed 18 January 2021.

Thoenig, J.C. (2005) Territorial administration and political control: decentralization in France, *Public Administration*, 83(3): 685–708.

Timmins, N. (2001) *The Five Giants: A Biography of the Welfare State*, London: HarperCollins.

Torrance, D. (2020) EU powers after Brexit: 'Power grab' or 'power surge'? Insight House of Commons Library, 29 July, https://commonslibrary.parliament.uk/eu-powers-after-brexit-power-grab-or-power-surge/, accessed 24 November 2020.

Trench, A. (1993) Legal aspects of subsidiarity in the United Kingdom, *Subsidiarity within the European Community: A Federal Trust Report*, London, 55–63.

Trench, A. (ed) (2007) Introduction, in A. Trench (ed), *Devolution and Power in the United Kingdom*, Manchester: Manchester University Press, pp 1–23.

Trench, A. (2015) *The Dynamics of Devolution: The State of the Nations 2005*, Luton: Andrews UK Limited.

Van Den Brande, L. (2014) *Multilevel Governance and Partnership: The Van den Brande Report*, Brussels: EU.

Van Der Zwet, A., Miller, S. and Gross, F. (2014) A first stock take: integrated territorial approaches in cohesion policy 2014–20, 37th IQ-Net Conference, European Policies Research Centre, University of Strathclyde.

Vaughn, A. (2020) England and Wales had most excess deaths in Europe's covid-19 first wave, *New Scientist*, 14 October, https://www.newscientist.com/article/2256986-england-wales-had-most-excess-deaths-in-europes-covid-19-first-wave/, accessed 28 January 2021

Wall, S. (2008) *A Stranger in Europe: Britain and the EU from Thatcher to Blair*, Oxford: Oxford University Press.

Wallace, H.S. (1973) *National Governments and the European Communities*, London: PEP.

Wardman, J.K. (2020) Recalibrating pandemic risk leadership: thirteen crisis ready strategies for COVID-19, *Journal of Risk Research*, 23(7–8): 1092–120.

Welsh Government (2020) Building better places: the planning system delivering resilient and brighter futures: placemaking and the Covid-19 recovery, July, https://gov.wales/sites/default/files/publications/2020-07/building-better-places-the-planning-system-delivering-resilient-and-brighter-futures.pdf, accessed 23 November 2020.

White, H. (2020) The extension of coronavirus powers and the 'Brady amendment', https://www.instituteforgovernment.org.uk/explainers/coronavirus-powers-brady-amendment, accessed 27 November 2020.

WHO (2012) *Addressing the Social Determinants of Health: The Urban Dimension and the Role of Local Government*, Geneva: WHO Regional Office for Europe.

WHO (2020) COVID-19 Strategy update, April 14, https://www.who.int/docs/default-source/coronaviruse/covid-strategy-update-14april2020.pdf?sfvrsn=29da3ba0_19, accessed 20 November 2020.

Wilke, M. and Wallace, H. (1990) *Subsidiarity: Approaches to Power-Sharing in the European Community*, London: Royal Institute of International Affairs.

Willett, J. (2016) Cornwall's devolution deal: towards a more sustainable governance?, *Political Quarterly*, 87(4): 582–9.

Williams, S. (2020) 'It was a total invasion': the virus that came back from the dead, *The Guardian*, 21 November, https://www.theguardian.com/science/2020/nov/21/it-was-a-total-invasion-the-virus-that-came-back-from-the-dead, accessed 22 November 2020.

Wilson, S. (2020) Three reasons why Jacinda Ardern's coronavirus response has been a masterclass in crisis leadership, *The Conversation*, https://pustaka-sarawak.com/eknowbase/attachments/1587707273.pdf, accessed 25 November 2020.

Wincott, D. (2017) Brexit dilemmas: new opportunities and tough choices in unsettled times, *British Journal of Politics and International Relations*, 19(4): 680–95.

Wincott, D. (2018) Brexit is re-making the UK's constitution under our noses, *LSE,* http://eprints.lse.ac.uk/91620/1/Wincott_Brexit-is-re-making_Author.pdf, accessed 1 November 2019.

Zimakov, A.V. and Popov, E.V. (2020) EU cohesion policy 2021–2027: new tools to foster European integration?, *Innovative Economic Symposium*, Cham: Springer, pp 148–56.

Zorzut, A. (2020) Downing Street bars Sunday Times journalists from posing questions during coronavirus briefing, *The New European*, 27 November, https://www.theneweuropean.co.uk/brexit-news/downing-street-bars-sunday-times-journalists-from-posing-questions-during-78740, accessed 25 November 2020.

Index